Alexander Bruno Hanschmann, Fanny Franks

The kindergarten system

Its origin and development as seen in the life of Friedrich Froebel

Alexander Bruno Hanschmann, Fanny Franks

The kindergarten system

Its origin and development as seen in the life of Friedrich Froebel

ISBN/EAN: 9783742891419

Manufactured in Europe, USA, Canada, Australia, Japa

Cover: Foto ©ninafisch / pixelio.de

Manufactured and distributed by brebook publishing software (www.brebook.com)

Alexander Bruno Hanschmann, Fanny Franks

The kindergarten system

THE
KINDERGARTEN SYSTEM:

Its Origin and Development

AS SEEN IN THE LIFE OF FRIEDRICH FROEBEL.

Translated and Adapted from the Work of

ALEXANDER BRUNO HANSCHMANN

For the use of English Kindergarten Students

BY

FANNY FRANKS

With an Appendix on "The Education of Man"

LONDON
SWAN SONNENSCHEIN & CO., Lim.
SYRACUSE, NEW YORK: C. W. BARDEEN
1897

Dedicated

TO

ENGLISH MOTHERS

PREFACE

I HAVE often wished to hand on to other students the benefit I myself derived from the reading of Hanschmann's *Life of Froebel*, for I know no other piece of Froebel literature that presents so complete an account of the progress and development of Froebel's educational thought.

I think it is a good thing for the student to see how, in his search for a scientific basis for the education of man, Froebel turns from the unpreparedness of the school-boy back to the earliest period of infancy, thence to the mother, and finally to the maiden, some day to become a mother.

It is also an excellent lesson for the young teacher to watch the care and conscientiousness with which this born educator prepares himself for his office.

It was my sense of its value that led me to obtain Mr. Hanschmann's permission to translate the book. The task has been a difficult one, however; for, in order to make the book practically serviceable for the Kindergarten student, I have had to recast, transpose, or shorten some passages, and omit others, which would either distract attention from the matter of main interest, or encroach on ground already covered by translations.

The chief omissions are the chapter on "The Education of Man," already published in English as a complete work, and certain passages that seemed to me to be too metaphysical or speculative for the probable reader of the book.

The curtailments consist chiefly in making as short as possible the account of certain periods of Froebel's life already in the hands of the English reader, and in giving here and there a summary, rather than the actual contents of a passage. These alterations, it is true, prevent my offering the book to the public as a translation pure and simple; on the other hand, I trust they do not obscure Mr. Hanschmann's view of the great educator, nor, what is still more important, Froebel's inner history and scientific theory of education.

Out of a large book I have made a small one, which, though far from being all I could wish, will, I think, fill up a little gap in the accounts we already possess of Froebel's life and work.

I should like here to acknowledge my obligations to Mr. Hanschmann for having allowed me to modify the book in this way, and also to those of my friends who have contributed notes and criticisms.

FANNY FRANKS.

13, YORK PLACE, W.

CONTENTS

First Part.

CHAPTER I.
CHILDHOOD AND YOUTH: 1782 TO 1799—OBERWEISSBACH—
STADT-ILM—NEUHAUS 1

CHAPTER II.
YOUTH: 1799 TO 1807—JENA—FRANKFURT . . . 14

CHAPTER III.
FROEBEL AND PESTALOZZI: 1807 TO 1811—FRANKFURT—
YVERDUN 36

CHAPTER IV.
THE UNIVERSITY—THE BATTLEFIELD—THE MINERALOGICAL
MUSEUM: 1811 TO 1816—GÖTTINGEN AND BERLIN . 56

CHAPTER V.
FROEBEL'S SCHOOL FOR BOYS: 1816 TO 1826—GRIESHEIM
AND KEILHAU 72

CHAPTER VI.
TROUBLED TIMES: 1826 TO 1829—KEILHAU—GÖTTINGEN . 104

Second Part.

CHAPTER VII.
SWITZERLAND: 1830 TO 1836—FRANKFURT—WARTENSEE—
WILLESAU—BURGDORF 117

CHAPTER VIII.
THE FIRST KINDERGARTEN: 1836 TO 1843—BLANKENBURG—
FRANKFURT—DRESDEN—LEIPZIG 143

CHAPTER IX.
THE FROEBEL PROPAGANDA IN GERMANY AND BELGIUM:
1843 TO 1849—DARMSTADT—LEIPZIG—DRESDEN . . 170

CHAPTER X.
FROEBEL THE APOSTLE OF WOMEN: 1849 TO 1851—MARI-
ENTHAL 188

CHAPTER XI.
LAST DAYS: 1851 TO 1852—LIEBENSTEIN—GOTHA . . 211

CHAPTER XII.
FROEBEL'S IMMEDIATE SUCCESSORS: 1852 TO 1874 . . 228

APPENDIX I.
FROEBEL'S "EDUCATION OF MAN" 239

APPENDIX II.
MME. DE PORTUGALL . . . 245

INTRODUCTION

It would hardly be fair either to Mr. Hanschmann or to myself to call this book an actual translation. It is rather an account of the contents of the book, with such omissions, curtailings, and transpositions as seem to me necessary to render the material practically useful to Kindergarten students and others interested in the newer and better ways of training young children.

It shows what kind of man Froebel was, and how he came to elaborate his system; indeed, his biography is made the medium for tracing the growth and development of the Froebel idea from its very beginnings down to the establishment of the first Kindergarten. Froebel's life naturally divides itself into four main periods—*i.e.*, the first fifteen years, during ten of which we have presented to us a thoughtful, sensitive child, suffering a good deal from mismanagement and want of management. But the boy has an affectionate nature, and is apt to look on the sunny side, and we find him settling down in the happiest way in the new home provided for him between his tenth and fifteenth years. He profits at once by the more congenial atmosphere and more favourable circumstances. And in the youth of fifteen we have a simple-minded, pious, aspiring, and nature-loving creature. He conceives of God as the origin of all that is good and beautiful, and of nature as the teacher of humanity. The beauty of the physical world not only propounds many problems for him, but so wins his heart that he determines to choose only such a career in life as shall permit of his intimate association with nature and natural objects.

The second period of his life covers the ten or fifteen years which may be called the "Sturm und Drang" period. He spends the whole of this time striving to find his natural vocation, and to prepare himself for it. This is the most interesting period of his life. From this to the full evolution of the Kindergarten idea occupies upwards of a quarter of a century, and furnishes us with a complete history of Froebel's educational thought from the beginning of his experience in teaching to the time when he first makes clear to the world his new system of education. He at once sees himself to be fitted for the office of teacher; but the more he studies the boys under his care, the more he realises the need of a wider culture and a deeper knowledge of human nature. Several times he interrupts his teaching in order to study such subjects as Natural Philosophy, Psychology, and

Pedagogy, because he feels that a more complete knowledge of man, and of his place in God's universe, is absolutely necessary for his work. When he is about thirty, circumstances make him the natural guardian of some young relatives, and he starts as an independent schoolmaster. He has discovered before this that much might be done to render young boys more fit than they generally are to profit by school education. He has also pondered much on the difference of energy and zeal they put into different employments. He determines to find out the secret of this good-will on the part of the child, and his experiments teach him much about boy nature. Careful observation leads to the discovery of a great gap in the training of the young, lying somewhere between the home and the school. He is impressed with the importance of the home training as giving the tone to the whole of the child's future; and since home training depends upon the mother, it is she who must learn to understand the aim and end of education.

The training of women is the crown of Froebel's work, and entirely absorbs the last fifteen years of his life. During this last period Froebel studies the mother's instinctive methods as carefully as he had previously studied the characteristic tendencies of childhood; and just as in the child he wishes to develop the best and highest of his qualities, in the same way with the mother his object is to make her consciously pursue her best methods for the training of her child. His persistent and continuous effort for the good of humanity presents to us a remarkable example of unity of life.

Froebel is a fairly complete representative of the pedagogic thought of his time. It is difficult to analyse his intellectual debt either to his predecessors or his contemporaries; but there is no doubt that he came strongly under the influence of the philosopher Krause, and still more strongly under that of the great teacher of modern times, Pestalozzi.

Froebel's attitude towards Education is rather that of the constructor than the critic. He is less concerned in condemning the wrong than in pointing out the right way. His object is to show how, by an improved system of training, man may become a more perfect being. In basing his system on spontaneous activity, he not only goes with the trend of the child's mind, and gets the benefit of his energy and will, but brings about a free and healthy physical, moral, and intellectual growth. Moreover, he agrees with his contemporary, Krause, that *life* and *living* are what concern the educator, and that an education which makes instruction its chief aim and end is not worthy the name.

Froebel's object is not to infuse "new life into old forms," but to give the child a completely fresh start. His system is as opposed to the old ways as possible. In making the nature of the child its centre, Froebel embodies the spirit of his time—rides, as it were, on the crest of a wave that was moving towards a new natural science and a new psychology.

Comenius, in his *Panegersia*, had insisted that the child should be educated from the cradle; Bacon, the real father of the Pestalozzi and Froebel schools, had shown the need for a thorough training of the senses as the gateway into the mind; Rousseau had eloquently preached the doctrine of nature; but no one had come so close to the little child as Froebel. It is as if he said, "Where thou goest, I will go"; hand in hand he goes with the child, fitting his steps to those of his small guide. No one had encroached so boldly on the woman's province as Froebel, or shown her so clearly the special nature of her work.

Just as Pestalozzi's great contribution to education was "Anschauung," or observation, thought and deed in their right order, Froebel's great and final contribution to Pedagogy was the doctrine of "Darstellung," or a varied expression of the inner self by spontaneous activity. It goes hand in hand with the great Pestalozzian principle, and at the same time starts a new psychology of the child. It utilises and brings into its service the child's sportiveness, imaginativeness, and love of production. It does not, as Mr. Herbert Spencer suggested, relegate the activities that serve for recreation and pleasure to the leisure moments of life, but embodies them as fundamental factors of education.

The child, like the savage, thinks of decoration, beauty, and brightness before it can possibly be impressed with utility; and Froebel goes with the stream of the child's inner life, and so advances more rapidly than did his predecessors in their utilitarian practices.

The great error of the old education was that it implied a similarity of method in the child and the adult. Froebel showed that the child sets about his work in a totally different way, and with a totally different object. He is not capable of the persistence, concentration, and energy implied in a perfect mastery within narrow limits, but he is well able to follow a variety of pursuits in his simple and natural way. This is the best way of promoting his general capability. A modern novelist says it little matters what we are taught to do after twelve. There is something of the Froebelian idea in this. In any case, Froebel thinks it an all-important matter that the child should do the right things before he is twelve.

PART I.

LIFE OF FROEBEL

CHAPTER I.

CHILDHOOD AND YOUTH.

1782 TO 1799. OBERWEISSBACH, STADT ILM, NEUHAUS.

The Home—Birth—Father—Loss of Mother—The Stepmother—Influence—Contact with Nature—Village Girls' School—Religious Worship—Idea of Sex—Discussions of Doctrine—Childish Troubles—Brothers' Intercession—Altered Conditions—Uncle Hoffmann—The New Home—Boys' School—Choice of Profession Apprenticeship—Studies—Conception of Nature—Plan of Study Jena the Goal—Father's Severity—Personal Appearance—The Return Home.

SCATTERED over the wooded hills along the Valley of the Saal, in Thuringia, are some half-dozen hamlets forming the village of Oberweissbach. Towering above one of the clusters of houses is the little church, which, at the beginning of the century, was the centre of the religious life of about five thousand souls. It was under the care of Pastor Johann Jacob Froebel. Opposite the church was the parsonage, surrounded by kitchen garden, courtyard and grass plots, but otherwise much shut in by buildings, hedges, and stacks. The country around is undulating and picturesque, and of a kind to make its impression on a sensitive and poetic nature; and certainly Pastor Froebel's motherless little boy may be so described. Friedrich Wilhelm August Froebel was born at the Parsonage of Oberweissbach on the 21st April, 1782. He lost his mother when hardly a year old, and up to the age of four was left to the intermittent care of the servants, with a very scanty amount of attention from the much-occupied pastor. His best friends at this time were his elder brothers; and it is from his letters to these, to the Duke of Meiningen, and later, to the philosopher Krause, that the following autobiographical sketch of his childhood and youth has been gathered. Referring to the early loss of his mother, he says, "When my dying mother gave me her last kiss, my young life was delivered over to the world with all its temptations and evils, and from that moment there arose within me a struggle with myself and the world, which cast a gloom upon my early years." The atmosphere of the home was extremely religious and serious, and the little boy, having neither mother nor companions of his own age to sympathise with his infant needs, hardly knew the meaning of childish play; so that the great treasure he has assured to generations of children was denied to himself. The stern control and repression which were considered necessary for his discipline threw him back upon himself, and thus his natural reserve was increased by a want of freedom in his home life. His shy and timid manner repelled those who had been the cause of it, and his faults were met by hard words and severe punishments.

One of the worst consequences of all this was that Friedrich became estranged from his father. Pastor Froebel was a man of intelligence and culture. He devoted himself with untiring energy to the affairs of his straggling parish, but had little time for the details of domestic government. The result was that the lonely little boy was almost fatherless as well as motherless.

When he was four years old his father married again, and for a time he was happier, for his stepmother treated him kindly.

After the birth of her own son, however, her manner to Friedrich became reserved and stern, even to the extent of addressing him in the third person,* and the little boy was practically alone again.

His physical surroundings were less unfavourable, for though he was not allowed to climb the neighbouring hills, and his outlook was limited to the garden and homestead, yet the bright sky and the pure air round his home had their effect upon him. Pastor Froebel was fond of his garden, and might be seen working at it with his boys in the early morning. Both he and his wife, too, were lovers of order and beauty, and the children had plenty of opportunity for the exercise of their intelligence and self-control in the constant reforms and improvements made in the home. Of Friedrich's brothers, two especially exercised an important influence on his future—Christoph, who from the first thoroughly believed in him, and Christian, who so substantially supported his educational scheme. We shall hear of these two again. The eldest brother, August, became a merchant, and died early. The youngest, Traugott,† took up the profession of medicine.

* To address someone in the third person is a mark of contempt, e.g., a beggar is often addressed as follows:—"Will he leave the courtyard at once, or I will give him in charge."
† His half-brother.

Friedrich's home was permeated by a somewhat narrow Christianity, and though the pastor followed the religious thought of his time, he was inclined to set a higher value on obedience and faith than upon intelligent enquiry. Morning and evening the members of the family were carefully instructed in the doctrines of Sturm, Stollikofer, and the like. On such occasions Friedrich was much impressed, and full of good resolutions, which, however, the carelessness of childhood prevented him from carrying out.

The pastor taught his elder boys himself, but he had not the patience to teach Friedrich, and not being on very friendly terms with the master of the village boys' school, he sent him to the girls' school. The teaching was good, and there was a spirit of neatness, order, and peacefulness in the school which was highly beneficial to Friedrich. He was soon promoted to work with the bigger girls. In this class he had to learn a whole hymn, while the little ones only learned a verse from the Bible. One or two of these hymns long remained in his memory, and served to comfort him in moments of perplexity and trouble. He attended church twice on Sundays, sitting in the choir, and taking much interest in his father's sermons, though he could not always understand the highly figurative language he used. He was often present during the instruction given to those preparing for confirmation, and would listen with no little awe to such expressions as "going to hell," "coming to Christ," etc., which were scattered through the exhortations addressed to the candidates. Thus there grew up in his mind a religious ideal, and a vague purpose of finding his way to the goodness and purity of a Christ-like life.

As he listened to the severe reprimands given by his father to the married couples who came to him with their disagreements, it struck him as a sad and regrettable thing that human beings alone in nature should be troubled with difference of sex. But here his brother Christoph came to his help. Seeing his delight at the crimson threads of the hazel-catkin, he pointed out to him the two kinds of blossom on the same plant. This discovery of sex in the vegetable world interested him extremely, and helped him a good deal in his childish attempts to bring some order and connection into the mass of objects he was so fond of collecting in and around the vicarage garden.

Another impression stood out in his memory. Many believed in those days, as indeed they have done in our own times, that the end of the world was approaching. Friedrich had a way of reassuring himself on this subject. "The human race," he said to himself, "will surely never perish till it has become as perfect as it is possible to become on earth; and surely the beautiful world cannot be destroyed till we human beings have learnt to understand it perfectly."

He would listen with great interest to the warm discussions on religious questions between his father and his eldest brother, then a student of theology, and as each clung obstinately to his opinions, Friedrich would come to the conclusion that there must be truth on both sides.

Thus, whilst a good deal of conflict was going on in the young child's mind, his conclusions were generally of a hopeful, if not optimistic character. The outward conditions of his life, however, were not such as to encourage him. Little attention was paid to his education. His faults were made unpleasantly prominent; and whenever disputes arose between him and his half-brothers he was condemned unheard. And there was no appeal against this injustice; for his father, who might have put matters right, was so overburdened with the care of his immense parish, that he could not investigate the representations made to him about his little boy, and consequently often did him injustice. This made Friedrich afraid of his busy father, and of the stepmother, who might have been his best friend, and the result was that he became constrained in their presence and appeared obstinate, and at times untruthful.

It was better for Friedrich when brother Christoph was at home to plead his cause, for he saw plainly both the good in the boy and the mismanagement from which he was suffering. Happily for the permanent development of the child's character, a change of conditions came to him with his tenth year.

In the summer of 1792 there came on a visit to the parsonage Friedrich's maternal uncle, Pastor Hoffmann, from Stadt Ilm, who saw at once the awkward position of his young nephew. He had been very fond of Friedrich's mother, and, pitying the boy, asked to have him at Stadt Ilm for a time. This offer was gladly accepted by the busy pastor, and by the end of the year Friedrich was installed in his new home, where, under the influence of kindly treatment, gentleness, and encouragement, he soon took heart again. And not the least valuable of these good influences was the trust and confidence shown him. At home he might hardly go out of sight. Here, to his great delight, he was allowed to ramble alone over hill and dale, and thoroughly explore the neighbourhood.

Stadt Ilm lies in the broad part of the valley of the Ilm (the river which flows through Weimar, and which, as Schiller says, " has heard many an immortal song "). This beautiful region now lay open before him; and he enjoyed to the full the freedom to wander about as he pleased.

Now, too, he was for the first time to have the advantage of associating with boys of his own age, being one of forty in the upper class of the grammar school. In the playground, it is true, he found himself both physically and mentally at a disadvantage.

The repressed life of his earlier years, together with his sensitive and reflective nature, little fitted him for the alertness, the presence of mind, and the physical skill and readiness required by games in the playground; and though he did his best to compensate for the intelligent skill and vigour of his companions by audacity and daring, it was some time before the boys permitted him to share their games as an equal. In the schoolroom he was dreamy and odd. The teachers failed to interest or stimulate him. Most of the subjects in the school were but indifferently taught; and there was no attempt at demonstrating in the concrete, nor at any connection in the studies, so that a good deal of the teaching was over his head, and left him indifferent and apparently lazy.

But he was always able to give a complete account of his uncle's gentle and inspiring sermons, and though the religious instruction he received at school was rather advanced and philosophical for so young a boy, his father's previous teaching enabled Friedrich to follow it with a fair amount of success.

The stories about Jesus touched and inspired him.

The only other subject in which he made any marked progress was arithmetic. Here he soon learned all his teachers had to teach. They acknowledged his talent for mathematics. In reality this subject interested him, because it helped to explain others that were more attractive to his mind. Latin was miserably taught, and the whole school was backward. In geography there was no attempt to connect that which had to be learned with what the boys already knew, nor to demonstrate objectively. There was just as little method in the teaching of the mother-tongue.

The boy's moral nature, however, expanded under the combined influence of his youthful companions, the peace and quiet of his uncle's home,* and the beautiful country surrounding it. The coercion and opposition from which he had suffered at home, had perhaps stimulated his originality and independence, and rather increased than diminished his reasoning power; and now that his energy was no longer required to overcome adverse conditions, it was set free to grapple with subjects which a less thoughtful child might have found repulsive. And though his school offered little stimulus for his observing powers, he explained many things to himself in his own way. In a letter to his brother some years later he says: "Thanks to my youth, and to the kindly influences that surrounded me, I enjoyed a freedom which resulted in an extension of my outlook, an increase of my strength, and in the natural development of my inner life. I had inherited from my mother a pure-minded simplicity and candour which, though it may occasionally have exposed me to

* Uncle Hoffmann's family consisted of himself and an aged mother-in-law.

temptation, yet had its effect in preserving me from serious evils."

He was allowed to stay with Uncle Hoffmann till after his confirmation. On his return home, at the age of fifteen, he was treated with less severity than formerly, and at once threw himself heart and soul into the busy life going on at the parsonage. His leisure moments were spent in his father's study, where he found to his great delight a map of the alphabets of all nations, on which he was able to trace the origin of the German written characters to an Asiatic alphabet. He found, too, in the library the story of Samuel Lawill, whose magic ring warned him by pressure when he was about to commit an unworthy act. Friedrich felt highly indignant when Samuel threw it angrily away because it hurt him.

Friedrich's confirmation being over, it was thought time to consider his future. His brothers were at the university preparing for professional careers. But, on account of the expense, it was thought unadvisable for Friedrich to go to college. His faculty for mathematics seemed to point to commerce, for which a mere smattering of Latin would suffice; and this could be acquired, it was thought, in the intervals of home occupations. But it may well be believed that this prospect was not one to satisfy the thoughtful, energetic boy. Moreover he had learned to love field and forest, and to value the opportunities for quiet contemplation, and the health and freedom of an outdoor life. He had, too, his own ideas about self-development, and believed that a life in the open air was conducive to nobility of character. The only result of his father's enquiries as to openings for

Friedrich was the offer of a secretaryship with a revenue officer, or, as an alternative, the position of page to a minister of State; neither of which was approved of. When at length the boy's own inclinations were consulted, he declared his wish to become an agriculturist. His ideas as to what this implied were somewhat vague. But he pictured to himself a combination of farmer, huntsman, overseer, accountant and land surveyor; and naturally concluded that the most direct way of becoming a first-rate agriculturist was to master each of these employments by turn. A knowledge of geometry and mensuration would be necessary; and he mentally added subjects adapted to self-improvement. In any case this plan offered the ambitious boy opportunity for contemplation and uninterrupted study. The premium required for his apprenticeship with a first-rate husbandman was beyond his father's means, but a forester, distinguished for his knowledge of geometry and valuation, expressed himself willing to take the boy, and an agreement was drawn up for two years. Friedrich was to live with this gentleman at Neuhaus, high up in the Thuringian Forest, and to receive instruction in forestry, mensuration, geometry, and valuation. The arrangements were completed by Midsummer, 1797, and the boy of fifteen and a half was dismissed by his father with the somewhat severe injunction that he was to bring home no complaints; they would not be heard, and he would only be condemned beforehand.

Friedrich had been told that it required a thoroughly efficient geometrician to be a successful agriculturist; and though geometry proper was an unknown subject to the young apprentice, he knew it was in some way connected with his favourite study arithmetic; and fired by the fascination of such magic terms as efficient mastery, valuation, meadow, forest, with all they implied, and unabashed by his father's parting words, he joyfully and resolutely started on his professional career. Alas! as far as his training was concerned, he was to be cruelly undeceived; for his master, though clever and accomplished himself, was entirely lacking in the skill and patience required for teaching others. The knowledge he had gained from his books was unavailing when an explanation was required. And in addition to this incapacity, he was so engrossed by business (especially some timber-floating he had undertaken) that he seldom had time or inclination to instruct his apprentice. Mostly he was away from home, and Friedrich had to depend on his own exertions for any skill or knowledge he wished to acquire. There were some excellent books on geometry and forestry in his master's library, and with these as companions, and Nature as his guide, our young enthusiast spent the first year of his stay at Neuhaus not so unprofitably as might have been expected. He lived practically alone, and became timid and reserved; but he looked upon Nature as his friend and comforter, and would spend hours examining and comparing plants, insects, or other objects found in field or forest. It was with childish delight that he pressed and arranged his botanical specimens, or classified his insects. He was proud to think that he, alone and unaided, had discovered their characteristics and their place in nature. In each new-found treasure he sought for some indication of the connectedness and unity of plan in the natural world, which even at this time he instinctively felt must be discoverable. He believed, too, that some noble purpose lay beneath these various forms, something higher than what was indicated by mere classification. A worthy student of nature should not merely collect facts, but should, he thought, be able to refer them to some deeper truth underlying them. Thus a certain conception of nature formed itself in his mind, and covered all that the word "agriculture" had previously conveyed to him. Henceforth his aim should be to study nature, which at this time did everything for him, whilst it seemed to him that man did nothing. Looking into his own mind he sought to understand the inner life and destiny of the human being, and realised more and more his want of self-knowledge and his inadequacy to solve the problems of nature. Fortunately for Friedrich, a young doctor, living in the neighbourhood, became interested in the boy's self-guided studies, and, observing his tendencies, urged him to take up seriously the study of Natural Science. This friend put into his hands a treatise on Botany.

Friedrich spent the last six months of his stay at Neuhaus in mastering the contents of this book, which in its turn suggested the following plan of study:—
1. Physical Geography, or the study of the earth. 2. Its direct productions, *i.e.*, such plants and animals as may be observable. 3. Mathematics, which hitherto had only covered the elements of arithmetic, geometry, and mensuration.

Friedrich had soon discovered, in his master's library, works on his favourite subject (mathematics) by Gerstenberg and Voigt. The interest of these works inspired our young agriculturist with an intense desire to study Natural Science under these eminent teachers, then at Jena. The course pursued by German youths at the gymnasium had no attraction for him. He had found school teaching very superficial and unattractive; moreover, the mere acquisition of knowledge was not his object. But he felt that it would be useless to endeavour to shorten his apprenticeship. He must complete his two years' course at Neuhaus.

There came to Neuhaus about this time a troupe of actors who gave a performance in the castle, and Friedrich went with his friend. He was much impressed, and went again and again, reflecting as he wandered home through the night on what he had seen. One evening, after a representation of Iffland's "Huntsman," he told one of the young actors that he regarded a profession capable of awakening such noble feelings in the human breast as most enviable. The young fellow, however, revealed to him the glamour surrounding the career of these wandering actors, and the misery that often lay behind it. And Friedrich became conscious of his own extreme immaturity. His father, to whom he innocently confided these experiences, reproached him bitterly for having visited the theatre, and it needed the intercession of brother Christoph to make peace between them.

The forester, though conscious that he had not done his duty by Friedrich, would have liked to keep him for another year after his apprenticeship was over (Midsummer, 1799). But Friedrich had Jena in his mind, and longed for more intellectual advantages. So he left at the appointed time, and cheerfully tramped homewards, trusting that some way of fulfilling his noble ambition would be found. Thus terminated his childhood and early youth.

CHAPTER II.

YOUTH.

1799 TO 1807. JENA, FRANKFURT.

New Troubles—Jena at last—Professor Batsch—Father's Death—Employment as Bailiff—Friends—Journey to Frankfurt—Brother Christoph's Encouragement—Recognition of Mission—Frankfurt Education *versus* Architecture—Loss of Testimonials—The Model Pestalozzian School—Pestalozzian Inspiration—First Visit to Yverdun—Pestalozzi's Methods—Tutorship—Educational Ideals—Vain Hope of University Study.

AN ardent wish is seldom unmixed with fear; and though Friedrich did not waver in his choice of a career which should be worthy of his best efforts, he anticipated a certain amount of opposition on the part of his friends. In order to meet this he went on his way home to consult with his brother Christoph, who had always done his best to cheer and encourage him. But he was shocked to find that Christoph had already received an account of his doings, which would certainly have prejudiced a less staunch friend against him. Pastor Froebel had forwarded to his eldest son a letter, in which the forester had accused Friedrich of having wasted his time at Neuhaus, and of being (in spite of the testimonial of efficiency he had given him on leaving) ignorant and unfit for his work.* But Friedrich gave his brother a full and candid account of his studies and of the way in which he had spent

* He knew little of Friedrich's assiduous private studies.

his time, and of the forester's neglect and indifference towards him; and when reproached by his brother for having kept silent about such treatment, he explained that when he left home his father had definitely warned him against making complaints.

The brothers hereupon wrote to their father a clear refutation of the forester's charges against Friedrich, and succeeded in reassuring him. For the present, however, he took no active measures for the boy's encouragement, whilst the stepmother openly defended the forester, and declared that Froebel would never do any good. With all this against them, the brothers realised that it would be useless to propose any plan of study for Friedrich which involved expenditure, and that for the present there was nothing to do but to wait.

All his aspirations after a noble and consistent life must be renounced. This was a dreary and discouraging moment for the ambitious boy.

> "Ach, aus dieses Thales Gründen,
> Die der kalte Nebel drückt,
> Könnt ich doch den Ausgang finden,
> Ach wie fühlt ich mich beglückt!
> Dort erblick ich schöne Hügel,
> Ewig jung und ewig grün!
> Hätt ich Schwingen hätt ich Flügel,
> Nach den Hügeln zög ich hin."

He had ventured to lift his eyes to Jena—the seat of learning—the scene of such labours as those of Voigt and Gerstenberg. But he hardly dare express his secret wish even to himself. Curiously enough, however, the chance of seeing the University came to him by a mere accident. It seems that his brother

Traugott, then a medical student at Jena, had urgent need of his allowance, and Friedrich, being the only unoccupied member of the family, was entrusted to carry it to him. It may be imagined with what an elastic step our youth set out on his travels along the beautiful valley of the Saal, past Ortamund and Kahla, towards the very centre of intellectual culture. On his arrival the brothers visited several of the colleges, and Friedrich was enchanted with the mental activity of the place, and soon confided to his brother his great desire for study. On re-entering Traugott's rooms, the two youths put their best efforts into a letter to Pastor Froebel, in which they begged his permission for Friedrich to stay at Jena during the eight remaining weeks of the term. They promised that the time should be used entirely for the benefit of his future career. To the boys' great delight, they received a favourable answer, and Friedrich at once began the study of topographical maps and charts and other subjects conducive to a knowledge of agriculture. He worked most assiduously till Whitsuntide, when the two brothers tramped home together. The stepmother at once congratulated Friedrich on being able at length to say that he had been "to college." But he was too happy to let this irony disturb him, and kept his object steadily in view.

Pastor Froebel had no wish to hinder his boy's studies as long as these could be carried on without trenching upon his pecuniary resources, and decided that a small legacy that was to come to him from his mother should be spent upon young Friedrich's studies at Jena. It was hoped this would suffice for several college terms. So with his second guardian's consent, our agriculturist, now seventeen and a half years old, returned to the University in time for the autumn term. A letter from his father, testifying to his capacity for the study of finance, exempted him from the matriculation examination, and he was at once admitted as a student of Natural Philosophy. The words "Philosophy" and "Science" had a strange, mysterious sound for this impressionable youth. Hitherto he had only thought of the practical side of his studies, and Natural Philosophy seemed like unattainable greatness to him. But the very words served to give a deeper meaning to his work. Jena was favoured at this time by the presence of three distinguished men:—Voigt, Professor of Mathematics; Batsch, Professor of Natural Philosophy and Medicine (whose botany class especially interested Friedrich); and Göttling, Professor of Chemistry.*

For the idea of evolution and continuity of plan in the animal world revealed to him by Professor Batsch, Froebel could never be grateful enough; and he listened to Batsch's demonstrations of the similarity in the skeletons of human beings, birds and fishes, with the most absorbing interest. Batsch's teaching sharpened his power of observation, and strengthened his love of nature. This professor introduced him to a scientific association, which very soon drew his tendency for research into its service by making him curator of its scientific specimens.

* (Johann Friedrich Voigt, 1751 to 1823, Professor of Physics and Mathematics at the University of Gotha, and subsequently at Jena in 1789. In 1774 Voigt published his Applied Mathematics, to be followed a year later by his Pure Mathematics.

Joh. Friedrich August Göttling, 1755 to 1809, came to Jena with Voigt.

August Johann Georg Carl Batsch, 1761 to 1802.)—K. M. CLARKE.

He found less connectedness and less interest in the lectures of the other professors. He enjoyed Göttling's experiments on chemical affinity, and Voigt's practical geometry, but he was little fitted to grapple with the more abstract subjects. He was but a simple, uneducated boy, with a self-taught smattering of this and that. He had a vague idea of Kepler's Laws of the Spheres, but had read none of the serious scientific works of his time. Hence he was little prepared for scientific study in the true sense of the word.

On his first arrival, like a starving man, he had devoured whatever mental food he could find, suitable or unsuitable; he had no one to advise him. Hence much of his time was at first wasted on subjects that might have waited, and his stay in Jena was not as profitable as it might have been. And by the time he was in the condition to profit by his studies a new trouble came upon him, in the shape of want of funds: not that he had in any way been careless or extravagant. His utmost indulgence was an occasional visit to the theatre, or a simple outing with his brother. Indeed he associated very little with the other students, being shy of their superior attainments. It was through his brother Traugott that he was now in trouble; for shortly after his arrival in Jena, Traugott had borrowed part of his small allowance, and had not returned it, so that by the end of the second term he found himself with an empty purse, and no prospect of help out of the difficulty.

The idea of quitting the University just as he was beginning to profit by his studies could only be a very last resource. He begged his father to come to his aid, but Pastor Froebel required much persuasion, and at length only consented on such conditions as were refused by his co-trustee. This delay increased Friedrich's difficulties, and he was reduced almost to despair. He had not yet paid his term's fees, and was afraid to face his fellow-students and teachers. At last the crisis was reached by a debt of 30 thalers due to a restaurant for food. The Senate, after several notifications to Friedrich, at length applied to his father, threatening the boy with imprisonment unless the account was paid. Each of the trustees wanted the other to pay it. The old pastor suggested that his co-trustee should hand up the small remainder of Friedrich's maternal legacy for the purpose, but this was illegal. So Friedrich was thrown into the debtors' prison, where he remained for nine long weeks. At length his father consented to make the necessary payments, but only on the condition that Friedrich should not expect him to leave him anything in his will. This renunciation having been signed by Friedrich, in the presence of the Senate of the University, he was released. The nine weeks spent in confinement had not been wasted. He had worked at Latin, which he hoped would help him with his scientific studies; had read Winckelmann's *Letters on Art*, and a translation of the *Zendavesta*, which did a good deal to broaden his ideas of religion. He also wrote a treatise on geometry, with a view to getting employment. The summer term of 1801 was his last at Jena. Referring to it some years after, in a letter to his brother Christoph, he says, "There is no doubt that I should have benefited more by my stay in Jena had I been well advised; yet I cannot say that it was of no advantage to me. I certainly came away with a better knowledge of my own resources and limitations; I had learned to know what I wanted; and was, in short, more matured. My world, as I conceived it, though not complete, was now something better than a collection of isolated facts; I had gained in width of view and definiteness of idea." The result was that Friedrich's ideal of his profession had expanded more and more, till it included the mastery of all the sciences on which agriculture is based.*

Immediately on being liberated from confinement he started for home. The beautiful Thuringian Forest, which was then in all the glory of spring (1801), had an exhilarating effect upon the youth of nineteen, so that, in spite of the discouragement and disapproval which probably awaited him at the parsonage, he was full of hope and good resolutions. His first step was to make a plan for further study. As a guide he took a synoptic chart of the arts, and determined to work up the different subjects by means of some scientific periodicals which he found in his father's library. Here, in his small bedroom, he would sit by the hour, covering folios of paper with different plans and time-tables, never being able to satisfy himself. His father finding him one day thus occupied, reproached him severely for wasting his time, and could not be persuaded to see the good that underlay this apparently useless occupation, till brother Christoph came home and interceded for him. The bulk of the pastor's library consisted of works on theology; but Friedrich found some gems of German literature. The two great German poets he only knew as yet by name. Shortly after his return home he obtained employment as

* For this appalling list see *Hanschmann*, p. 21.

practical assistant to a farmer at Hildburghausen; but he had hardly had time to settle down to his work when he was recalled by his father's sudden illness. And perhaps the next few months (*i.e.*, from November, 1801, to February, 1802, when his father died) was the only period of mutual confidence and understanding between the upright, well-intentioned old pastor and the young son, who, in spite of all misunderstandings, so thoroughly honoured and appreciated him.

Our youth of twenty had now only himself to depend upon. At Easter he undertook the temporary management of an estate near Bamberg, in Bavaria. His duties were light and chiefly secretarial, and left him plenty of leisure for study or for the exploration of the beautiful neighbourhood. Here, again, he found a good library, and he had a most congenial companion in the family tutor. This gentleman introduced him to the doctor, the clergyman, and some of the professors in Bamberg. And in the spring of 1803 he moved into the town with a view to getting an engagement of a more practical nature. But his youth and want of experience stood in his way, and he was glad to obtain a little chart-drawing, and to survey a small estate belonging to a gentleman he had met at Jena. This gentleman was a disciple of Schelling, and Friedrich and he had many discussions on matters of natural philosophy and art. He also introduced him to Bruno's *Weltseele*.

At length, in February, 1804, in answer to an advertisement, Friedrich was offered an appointment as private secretary to Herr von Dewitz, a magistrate at Gross-Milchow (Mecklenburg-Strelitz), which he was glad to accept. Before beginning his work he paid a visit to his uncle at Stadt-Ilm. Uncle and nephew much enjoyed their mutual reminiscences of his stay at Ilm. His uncle told Friedrich that the five happy years he had spent at Ilm were due to his great affection for his sister (Friedrich's mother), and it touched him a good deal to think of the influence his dead mother had thus exercised over his life.

Having, whilst at Bamberg, learned a new method of book-keeping, he was able to use it at Mecklenburg for the benefit of Frau von Dewitz, who, however, was herself a most accomplished accountant. The family tutor introduced him to several good families in Mecklenburg; but the strongest influence on him at this time was that of Professor Wollweide, a young doctor from Göttingen, who had come to spend the holidays with the two eldest sons of Herr von Dewitz, whom he was coaching at Halle.

Doctor Wollweide, who later on distinguished himself in physics and mathematics, was the means of drawing Friedrich's attention once more to these formerly beloved studies. He now learned to apply mathematics to building, and under the doctor's direction procured some excellent works on architecture.

This subject so charmed him that he determined to take it up in good earnest, and soon learned to regard architecture as a nobler profession even than agriculture. Amongst the works that served further to stimulate his self-culture and to extend his ideas were Proeschke's *Anthropological Fragments*, and the writings of Novalis and Arndt. Proeschke impressed him with the importance for the human being of environment; Arndt with the relationship which the individual bears to the community, the nation and the world; and

Novalis taught him to know himself and the meaning of his aspirations. He brought away from this reading an altogether new conception of life. He says: "Through the knowledge of myself I was learning to know all men. Step by step my experience was teaching me the macrocosm through the microcosm." He now threw himself with the utmost vigour into all that tended towards his own culture. His desire was to obtain employment which would increase his knowledge of architecture and the allied subjects, and so fit him for what he now regarded as his future calling. He wrote to his tutor friend in Bamberg asking whether Frankfurt would not be a likely place for the work he had in mind. His friend, who had spent some years in Frankfurt, approved of the suggestion, and proposed their meeting there in the summer, and endeavouring on the spot to realise Friedrich's plan.

Friedrich had already obtained his release from his engagement with Herrn Dewitz, and decided to proceed to Frankfurt at once. He wrote with some diffidence to his favourite brother, fearing his disapproval of the frequent change of plans, but telling him of his "irresistible impulse towards self-improvement." When the answer came he was afraid to open it, and only did so after the suspense had become intolerable. The letter both saddened and relieved him. His brother wrote most sympathetically about his future, but gave him the sorrowful news that his beloved uncle at Ilm had passed away. He had left to his nephew Friedrich and to each of his brothers a small legacy. Thus Friedrich was able to carry out his plan.

Full of life and new courage he started for Frankfurt. On his way he spent some delightful May days in the country home of a friend at Ackermark. Gladly and hopefully the young dreamer sped through the beautiful grounds that led to the house. Field and flower-bed glistened beneath the early dew, the beauty of his native soil touched him. "The more closely we unite ourselves to Nature," he thought, "the more does she reveal to us."

A few words, written in his friend's scrap-book on leaving, show that even at this time, though unconsciously, he was at heart seeking a larger and wider sphere even than architecture. "You," he wrote, "with your fruitful land, give men the possession of their daily bread; let my object be to give them the possession of themselves."

From Ackermark he wandered in the lovely May weather through the Thuringian Forest and mountains to Griesheim, of which his brother Christoph was pastor. Here his plans for self-education met with the fullest encouragement, for brother Christoph had himself experienced the disadvantages of repressed youthful aspirations. He sympathised heartily with Friedrich's life and vigour. "Be faithful," he said, "to your own heart," and he wrote the following words in Friedrich's scrap-book: "Struggle and strife is the lot of aspiring men. Only be firm and strong, face your difficulties manfully, dear brother, and you will reach the goal." These were golden words for our eager youth, and they served not a little to brace and support him in this moment of anxiety and suspense, and to send him on his way strengthened and refreshed.

YOUTH. 25

As he tramped along the road towards the Wartburg, the idea which had suggested itself to him at Ackermark recurred to him, that his mission was to restore to man the peaceful possession of his own soul. He felt there must be some beautiful and simple way of freeing human life from the strife and contradiction with which it is weighted. Cheered and solaced by the beautiful journey, and by the hope of a speedy fulfilment of his desires, he reached Frankfurt on Midsummer Day, 1805, and found his friend awaiting him. Frankfurt, one of the six free cities of Germany, the birthplace of the poet Goethe, was at this time one of the most important centres of social, political, and intellectual life.

Friedrich soon obtained employment with an architect. But architecture was rather a means of culture than an end in itself. Imperceptibly and unconsciously he was turning from the building of houses towards the building of men. Through architecture an æsthetic feeling might be awakened in man, but for his general culture and for the ennobling and perfecting of humanity more was necessary.

There had come to Frankfurt a little before this one of the most enthusiastic disciples of Pestalozzi, Gottlieb Anton Gruener (1778-1844). He was now principal of a most successful Pestalozzian Institution, and Friedrich was introduced to him and his teachers. They met often, and had many lively discussions about education. Friedrich candidly confessed his new ideas and aspirations, and Gruener, who had sufficient knowledge of men to understand the earnest and enthusiastic nature of his new friend, exclaimed, "Give up your architecture; that is not your work. You must become an educator. We want a teacher in our school. If you will come the post shall be yours."

Our young architect was much startled by so sudden a proposition, for though his thoughts had been tending more and more in the direction of education, it had not occurred to him to regard himself as having any practical connection with it. He was much impressed, however, and reflection showed him that both his inner life and his outer conditions pointed in this direction, and helped to decide his fate. Gruener's offer was genuine. His friend advised him to accept it. The magic name "Pestalozzi" sounded like a distant echo.

He called to mind an occasion on which his father had read an extract from the newspaper about a man, living in a secluded village in Switzerland, who had taught himself to read, write, and cipher at the age of forty.* And this had comforted him at times when his own education appeared to be so unsatisfactory.

The second teacher in Gruener's school, Naenni, had been with Pestalozzi at Burgdorf, contemporaneously with Niederer and other well-known teachers. Gruener

* This "man" cannot have been Pestalozzi, for he was a distinguished student at the University of Zurich when that University was one of the first in Europe. One well-known fact will show his position there: His Greek professor published a translation of some portion of the orations of Demosthenes. Pestalozzi says he "had the boldness" to compete with his professor, and with such success that the University published his translation. He may have been a very poor Greek scholar, but he had some literary ability. Later in life he gives another illustration of it, when he revised the revision of "Leonard and Gertrude." His translation served for preface to his earliest work, "Agis," and is included in Seyffarth's edition. If "the man" referred to is Pestalozzi it only shows that newspaper reports misrepresented him then, as our writers and teachers do to-day. (Note by Mr. E. Cooke, author of English version of Pestalozzi's *How Gertrude Teaches her Children*.)

gave Froebel a pamphlet he had written entitled *Letters from Burgdorf about the Pestalozzian methods and institution.* He informed Froebel that he had gone to Switzerland for a holiday and rest after his training as tutor and class teacher, and had made his visit to Burgdorf with the idea of refuting the new-fangled, much-vaunted Pestalozzian methods, which appeared to him to be a relapse into barbarism. But lo! he had found that this very method was the best cure for existing evils in education; so that the intended scoffer had become a most enthusiastic disciple. He had come to curse, but remained to pray.*

All this had its influence on Froebel, but perhaps the circumstance that finally determined him to become a school teacher was the loss of his college certificates and testimonials. This misfortune had, as it were, cut him adrift from his past, and though he had not at this time abandoned the idea of making a special study of mathematics, he was glad to accept the post of assistant in Gruener's model Pestalozzian school. "It is as a mathematician and scientist that I shall win my freedom," he writes in 1805, "for that way lie all my tendencies and inclinations." Behind

---

* In his *Main Principles underlying the Science and Art of Education*, Gruener expounds fully the Pestalozzian doctrine of Anschauung. Since then he had been an earnest advocate of the Pestalozzian system, as all his publications testify. But for a reform in national education he always maintained that practice went further than theory. "It wants something," he said, "besides literature and books if we are to reform our national education. The poor twenty-four written symbols of language and thought are insufficient to represent the world and all it contains. What we want is not words, but things, and their immediate effect upon us. We must cultivate perception, sense-impression, individual judgment, in short Anschauung."

this expression of his determination there lurked a dim consciousness that there was for him something higher and nobler than mathematics or science.

The very day after Gruener's offer Friedrich entered the school-room as class teacher, and, strange to say, he felt at once that here was the work for which he was best fitted. His class consisted of thirty or forty boys of nine to eleven years of age. The description of his feeling from the first moment in which he faced his boys is most refreshing. He writes to his brother (end of August, 1805): "I felt like a fish in water, a bird in the air, perfectly at home in my work, and as if I had always been a teacher. Indeed it was as if I had never wished for anything else, and yet, before I entered that school-room I had never dreamed of such a thing as possible for me. Now I know I am in my element in the class-room; I cannot tell you how quickly and pleasantly the time flies; I love the children and they love me, and we quite look forward to the lessons. This happiness is no doubt partly due to my sense of the noble end towards which I am striving, but the mutual affection between myself and the children contributes its part." Thus his long-cherished ideals took shape, and gladdened him with feelings hitherto unknown; for though as yet unconsciously to himself, he had entered upon his mission.

In order to put him into the way of acquiring a theoretical knowledge of education, Gruener gave him Pestalozzi's *Essays on the Progress of Education in Switzerland*, and a biography of the great Swiss reformer. In this way Pestalozzi became the inspirer of his work, his teacher, and his pattern. He felt he must see this man with his own eyes; and taking advantage of the short holiday at the end of the term, he went to Yverdun, where his letters of introduction procured him a most hearty welcome.

The Bernese Government had decided to use the Castle of Burgdorf as offices. Muenchenbuchsee was offered to Pestalozzi instead, but here De Fellenberg would have had the chief direction, and to this Pestalozzi could not agree. Hence he had, in August, 1805, accepted the invitation to move his institution to Yverdun, on the Lake of Neuchatel. He carried with him one or two teachers and eight pupils. Froebel had now the opportunity of seeing an educational institution which was the embodiment of a great idea. The classes were freely open to him, and Pestalozzi and his teachers were always ready to give him help or information. His first impression was one of bewilderment. He was as yet hardly in a position to judge of the time-table and methods of such an institution as Pestalozzi's. He arrived at an unquiet moment for the institution. The Prince of Hardenberg had been commissioned by the Austrian Government to report on it, and there seemed to be a want of harmony and co-operation amongst the teachers, which may have been due to the agitation of the moment.

Some of the teaching fairly dazzled him by its rapidity and apparent success (*c.g.* Kruesi's Arithmetic). Geography was treated too mechanically, though it was taken by a spirited young teacher (Tobler). Of nature-teaching Froebel only heard Botany, which was undertaken by another clever teacher (Hopf), who had a method of his own. At every discoverable point in the lesson, *e.g.* the position of the leaves or of the flowers, he would let the pupils discuss all the forms they knew, so as to emphasize the point then before them. This principle interested Froebel very much, but he thought there was something almost disturbing in its application. The language-teaching in the school was, at this time, wanting in system. Music was taught from figures,* and reading from Pestalozzi's A B C.† The simultaneous class-teaching he thought admirable, as it allowed every pupil to take the grade for which he was best fitted in each subject. The time-table did not seem to him as all-round as he could have wished, many important subjects being overlooked.

Froebel says that Pestalozzi himself seemed to be almost bewildered by the mental machinery of the place. He never could give any account of his methods; he used to say, "Come and see, it goes grandly."

Froebel's short visit came to an end about the middle of October; he carried away the following few words in the handwriting of Pestalozzi: "By thought and speech is your road prepared, but silent action alone will enable you to reach the goal."

Froebel returned to Frankfurt about the middle of October, 1805, by which time Gruener's negotiations with the Council at Frankfurt had brought about his appointment as permanent teacher. There were at this time two hundred children in the school, five boys' and three girls' classes, together with four per-

---

* The Chevé system, invented by Rousseau.

† See an account of this in Dr. Wichard Lange's edition of Froebel's Pedagogic Works, vol. i.

manent and nine visiting teachers. Froebel was entrusted with the re-organisation of the school. He took up his work with the utmost spirit and resolution, and though his management made great demands on the devotion of the teachers, his influence was declared by the authorities to be of the utmost value to the school, and to work wonders amongst the children.

Froebel was careful never to puzzle his pupils with anything he had not first thoroughly worked out himself; and in a school where method was regarded as of the utmost importance, his originality and resource met with the keenest appreciation. His class soon became the show class of the school. His first public examination was a brilliant success. He gave a lesson on Physical Geography, under the head of "Heimathskunde" (*i.e.*, study of environment), a subject recently introduced into the school. Froebel took this opportunity of showing how easily and well the pupil may learn from direct contact with natural objects and surroundings; and how, by proceeding in a gentle and orderly manner from the near to the more remote, he may make his own what no books can teach. His pupils demonstrated well the value of their little voyages of discovery, and also the beneficial influence exercised upon them by one who loved Nature for herself, and made a thorough study of whatever he put before his pupils.

That they had most carefully studied the plants, animals, hills, dales, rivers, mountain streams, rocks, and other features of the country round Frankfurt, was evident; and that the facts thus discovered by themselves were utilised for their benefit in the school-room was equally evident.

Froebel placed a blackboard flat upon the floor, and with the help of the boys traced upon it the course of the River Maine. The position of Frankfurt being determined, he traced round it a line limiting the area to be taken in the lesson. From this starting-point the boys proceeded to fill in the features of the locality which had come under their direct observation (*i.e.*, roads, hills, streams, buildings, etc.). When the picture was complete it was set up, and the boys were allowed to copy what they themselves had put together. They were then questioned by the teacher, and their ready answers showed how thoroughly they had mastered their own locality. "That is the way to learn geography," said the listeners. Other lessons followed, such as arithmetic, drawing, and language; to all of which he applied the Pestalozzian system in his own way. In the writing lesson (given to the girls) correct speaking was the basis of correct writing. The great success of this demonstration only served to inspire Froebel more than ever with the wish to perfect himself in educational methods. However pleasing his teaching was to others, he himself knew well how far short he fell of his own standard of efficiency, and he now determined to take the first opportunity of making a special study of Pedagogy.

In addition to his school work he was acting as private tutor to the three young sons of Herr Holzhausen, and this new work had further revealed to him the great difference between the introspective attitude of mind required for self-development, and the pedagogic point of view necessary for the education of others. Froebel was much interested in these boys, but he did not consider himself fitted for private teaching.

Their mother, however, had many serious and anxious talks with him about her boys, especially the two eldest, who had been under bad influence; and she pleaded so hard for his co-operation, and showed such confidence in his judgment, that he ended by undertaking to give them lessons in arithmetic and their mother-tongue, and to share their walks. Frau von Holzhausen's kindness, intelligence, and refinement, her simplicity and dignity of character, won Froebel's admiration, and a lasting friendship grew up between them. The way in which this noble woman overcame prejudice, opposition and hindrances of every kind, in order worthily to fulfil her duties as wife and mother, seemed to Froebel little short of heroic. His intercourse with Frau von Holzhausen served to impress him with his own want of culture. In his practice as a teacher he had had remarkable success; but, far more than this, practical ability was necessary if he was ever to become a true educationist.

His recent experience had convinced him that education was his life work, and worthy of his utmost devotion, and now it only remained for him to take up the study of pedagogy in all seriousness. For this purpose he proposed, firstly, to attend one of the universities for a year (either at Heidelberg or at Goettingen); secondly, to study such methods as those of Tillich, Plamann, and Arndt; thirdly, to go for one year to Yverdun, and finally to start a boys' school in accordance with his ideal somewhere in the

North of Germany. Gruener, seeing the eagerness with which he pursued his plan of development, had arranged to set him free at the end of two, instead of the three years agreed upon.

A few extracts from a letter, dated March, 1807, will show the unusual depth of thought and seriousness of this young man of five-and-twenty. "The object of education," he says, "is the realisation of a perfect humanity. Purity and simplicity of heart are as important for the educator as knowledge and culture; for it is the destiny of man that concerns him far more than his learning. Experience must be tested by scientific study and observation. Hence the pedagogue must study his subject from a philosophical, as well as from a practical point of view. He must make a special study of the physical, mental, and moral nature of man, and his place in the world. He must take anthropology and physiology into his service. The educator must himself be educated."

Froebel was conscious of his power to set before his pupils an ideal of humanity, and he now wanted to fit himself for helping them to reach this ideal. His love of nature, and also of self-culture, seemed to be but different forms of a deeper and larger love, *i.e.*, the love of humanity. His real aim from the beginning, though unknown to himself, had been the understanding and perfecting of the human being.

"I would have men," he cried, "who stand rooted in the world of nature, but who, with heads erect, can read the secrets of heaven; who cherish in their hearts the manifold beauty of earth, and the peace and calm of heaven—God's earth and God's heaven."

A gifted sage and thinker of our time,
Believer in humanity sublime,
Has thus described the man he wished to see,
Divine, yet human ; bound, yet ever free.

Erect he stands with dignity of stature,
With foot implanted in the world of Nature,
With head uplift, and clear and steady gaze,
He dares his piercing eye to heaven to raise.

To him all Nature's wealth of hue and form,
Her cloud and sunshine, mountain, sea, and storm,
Her ever changing mood, her smile, her tear,
Are revelations intimate and clear.

To such a man there is divinely given
The secret of the peace and calm of heaven.
His human heart holds sacredly enshrined
Such gladness as the pure on earth may find.

A human gladness and a heavenly joy,
A peace which nothing earthly can destroy—
The peace of heaven and joy of earth combined :
These would I in each human being find.*

* I have always been much impressed with this thought of Froebel's ; but offer the above versification for what it is worth.

CHAPTER III.

FROEBEL AND PESTALOZZI.

1807 TO 1811.   FRANKFURT, YVERDUN.

Froebel's Life with his Pupils—Gardening—Froebel an unconscious Follower of Rousseau—Value of the Joyousness of Childhood—Origin of the Kindergarten Occupations—Yverdun—Pestalozzi's Influence—Introduction of his System into Prussia—Failure in the midst of Success—Situation of Yverdun—Daily Routine—Pestalozzi and his Teachers—Froebel's Conception of Pestalozzianism—The Mother's Book—Sense Impressions—Movement—Sound—Number—Geography—Mathematics—Music—Drawing—Writing and Reading—Froebel's Criticisms—School Organisation—Home Education—Education of the Parent—History—Germs of the Froebel Idea—Pestalozzi's Religious Teaching—Dissensions at Yverdun—Public Examination of the Pestalozzian Institution—Froebel's Departure from Yverdun—Nature Studies.

THE third period of Froebel's history begins in a lonely cottage on a heath outside Frankfurt. Here he settled down, in July, 1807, as private tutor to the three sons of Herr von Holzhausen. He had been asked to try and find a tutor for them, but hitherto had been unsuccessful, and both he and Frau von Holzhausen at length gave it up in despair. Froebel, who was much attached to the boys, and sympathised with the mother's anxiety, after much conflict with himself, determined to give up the University for the present and undertake the boys himself. Gruener, who had set him free so that he might have scope for the self-culture he needed, disapproved of this reforging of the chains of bondage, and tried to dissuade him. But Froebel could not resist the pleading of mother and sons for his help. At the same time he was fully conscious of his incompetence to reach the standard he himself had fixed for the educator.

In a letter to his brother Christoph (probably on the subject of the Holzhausen tutorship), he writes: "A natural simplicity and purity of character is more valuable for the educator than a vast amount of worldly culture. Science points out the right road; experience must be tested by science; science leads through ideas back to idealised realities; pedagogy, though independent of philosophy, is closely connected with it. Philosophy indicates the principles of all science, and proceeds from the destiny of man back to the education he requires to fulfil it, and thus enlightens the views, and ennobles the work of the educator. He must base his operations on physiology and anthropology. General culture, *i.e.* a knowledge of nature, is assumed in the educator. He must study these subjects as well as ethics, languages, history, geography, method, and pedagogy."

It was with a sense of great responsibility that he took up his abode with the boys in their solitary little cottage. Like Pestalozzi and Rousseau, he had great faith in the influence of nature on the human mind, and this belief had certainly been verified in his own case. He felt also that the first thing to do was to free these boys from the trammels of convention and old associations, and to get complete control over them. This accomplished, it would be time to consider the means and methods of educating them. He determined from the beginning to share their life, amusements, and occupations, and to make everything contribute to their development. "The best education I can give them is to live with them," he said to himself. It was not always easy to harmonise and connect the subjects of study, but he was stimulated and encouraged in his search for unity of plan by the writings of such men as Seiler and Jean Paul Richter, in whose *Levana* he found much inspiration. Froebel enjoyed the peaceful, undisturbed life they led together, and gave himself up to the boys with a devotion to which he looked back in after years a little wistfully. This complete surrender of himself satisfied his instincts as an educator, and taught him many a valuable lesson. At first he trusted almost entirely to the influence of rambles in the fresh air, during which the boys were encouraged to take an interest in natural objects. Then their father gave the boys a piece of land, which the new colonists set to work with the most lively interest to turn into a garden. There was great rejoicing over each new plant, and many were the offerings of vegetable, fruit, or flower, the children made to parents or teacher. Froebel saw in their delight and interest in flowers a pledge of goodness, and a proof of the benefit of their contact with nature. But this wealth of happiness in early life suggested to him the sad reflection that "childhood and youth are ever unconscious of the riches they possess, only understanding their real wealth after they have lost it." "Will the time never come," he asked, "when youth may profit by the experience and wisdom of age? Of what service is this wisdom if it be only carried to the grave?"

Without being fully acquainted with Rousseau's works, Froebel carried out his main principle of leaving children time for self-education.' "Perfect growth," says this apostle of nature (Rousseau) "can only be attained through an entirely free development. That which a child cannot perceive by his senses, that which he cannot see to be either useful or pleasurable, vanishes away like chaff in the wind. Much of nature and little of books, more reality and less instruction, this is the education that in every period has brought forth the best men. A child must first learn to know the earth, the plants, the animals, and the human beings on its native soil before it can understand the more remote and distant places of the earth. Any other way will only produce parrots. A good education consists less in the dictation of what is good, true, and beautiful, than in the practice of it. What we have to do for early education is not so much to teach virtue and truth, as to protect the heart from evil and the mind from error." This was the task Froebel had set himself, and when in any difficulty about the eldest boy, he would simply follow the lead of the two younger boys, and trust to a simple life in nature.

The more he recalled his own early experiences, the more convinced he felt that the best basis for a good Christian life is a thoroughly happy childhood. He abstained from imposing on these children the religious forms which had had so deep a meaning for himself, trusting that nature would be his best helper.

The boys' gymnastics consisted chiefly of their daily rambles with their teacher, skipping, walking on stilts, and playing at ball. As the winter came on, Froebel felt the need of some indoor exercises. Again he recalled his own favourite employments as a child, and set himself to invent all he could think of.

Amongst these were drawing and designs on chequers, perforating paper or cardboard, cutting and weaving paper, geometrical cardboard-work, and wood-work. Indeed there is little doubt that here, with these three Frankfurt boys, he laid the foundation of what we now know as Kindergarten occupations. These he shared with the boys. "There seems," he writes, "to be something peculiarly gratifying to the young mind in production, and in the handling and transforming of material." He had not as yet begun to consider the cause of this satisfaction. At the same time he realised that some regular plan of study must be entered upon before the boys could attend a public school; and, doubting his own fitness to undertake the whole responsibility of this more advanced teaching, he once more turned his eyes in the direction of Pestalozzi.

The school at Yverdun was at this time at the very height of its renown; pupils were flocking thither from all parts of the world; and Froebel conceived the plan of placing the education of the boys in the hands of the great teacher, and, whilst superintending their studies, of perfecting himself in the Pestalozzian methods. Having obtained the consent of their parents, he carried the boys to Yverdun in the summer of 1808. He was full of hope and expectation, believing that there was no educational problem that could not be solved at Yverdun. His former stay with this great man had been too short to give him anything like a thorough insight into his scheme of education, but now he hoped to find there all that he was seeking. All that he had heard or read of Pestalozzi since his previous visit had but tended to increase his admiration. He felt sure thát his boys would come under a strong spiritual influence at Yverdun, and would have developed in them an all-sided activity and skill which would satisfy the utmost demands of their nature.

It was during the previous winter that the great philosopher, Fichte, had pronounced his celebrated "Appeal to the German Nation." In this speech, which resounded throughout Germany, he pointed specially to Pestalozzi. "This man," he declared, "in his idea of sound national education, held the secret of the 'new birth of the German nation'; he was the link in the history of the world between the old education and the new, and his was the only method calculated to enable the nation to satisfy his (Fichte's) demands. Our laws, our alliances, and the use to which we are to put our fighting power, are taken out of our hands," he cried, "but our education has not been thought of; if we want something to do, let us attend to that. Probably we shall be left undisturbed in that matter. Our only hope lies in education."

Queen Luise was greatly interested in education, and steadfastly supported Fichte's recommendations for its amelioration. She had learned at the enlightened court of her father in Mecklenburg-Strelitz to identify herself with all that concerned the national good. She had a thorough belief in Pestalozzi, and had been the means of sending several young Prussians to Yverdun to train. She rejoiced at the appointment of Pestalozzi's friend, Nikolovius, as minister, and wrote: "Frederick II. conquered provinces; Frederick William III. will conquer intellectual territory for his country." An entry in her diary in 1807 further illustrates her admiration of Pestalozzi: "I am reading *Leonard and Gertrude,*" she writes, " a book for the people, by Pestalozzi. If I could follow my own inclination, I would drive straight to Pestalozzi and thank him with tears for his great love of humanity."

The Chancellor von Tuerk, author of the *Letters from Muenchen Buchsee,* had himself studied with Pestalozzi at Burgdorf.

The Prussian Minister of Education, Von Altenstein, wrote to Pestalozzi in September, 1808: "Being thoroughly convinced of the value of the method of teaching which you have originated, and which you carry out so well, I have determined to introduce it into the elementary schools of Prussia, and thus bring about a thorough reform in school organisation, which I feel persuaded will have the best possible influence on the education of the people. The young men to be sent to you are to learn the principles of your education directly from yourself. And it is not intended that they should get a mere smattering of it, but they are to learn all the subjects, and to understand their various connections. They are to practise these different methods under the immediate guidance of their author and his efficient assistants; and I feel sure that the association with such workers will not only advance them intellectually, but, by persuading them of its sanctity, will prepare them morally for their educational office. May you be able to inspire these young teachers with the zeal which impels you to devote your life to the cause of education." The favour thus shown to Pestalozzi by those in authority naturally increased his popularity, and the result was that during the years 1808 and 1809 the establishment at Yverdun was overcrowded. People of all nationalities hastened to Switzerland to learn from this apostle of threescore years.

All classes in Prussia were at this time impressed with the importance of education. Statesmen and legislators shared the general enthusiasm. Freiherr von Stein* declared that the future of the nation would depend upon the educational system now to be decided upon, and urged the adoption throughout the country of Pestalozzi's methods. Pestalozzi held the secret of spiritual influence, and of the development of faculty in accordance with the nature of man. It was time for the Prussian nation to give up all narrow and one-sided systems which overlooked and neglected the very faculties and tendencies on which the dignity and power of the nation depended.

Froebel's second visit to Yverdun took place at the moment of its highest success. The institution numbered at that time about two hundred of various nationalities, and visitors came every day to see or to learn of the famous master. This mark of the general interest shown in his work filled Pestalozzi with gladness and hope. He had as yet no suspicion of approaching misfortune.†

---

* Minister of Public Instruction.

† This view is not generally accepted, as will be seen from the following passage taken from Mr. John Russell's Translation of Guimps' *Life of Pestalozzi* (Sonnenschein): "At the end of 1807, when the establishment at Yverdun was at the zenith of its fame, and exciting the admiration of scholars and sovereigns; when it was attracting crowds of pupils, disciples and visitors from every country, and filling everybody connected with it with joy and hope, one man alone was dissatisfied, one man alone saw that it could not endure, that it was doomed, like a plant at whose root there gnaws an undying worm. This man was Pestalozzi himself."

But in spite of the apparent success of the school, the seeds of dissolution were already ripe within it. It was the very overcrowding into the institution of large numbers that brought about its ruin. "Parents who were entirely ignorant of Pestalozzi's aim, eagerly demanded that their children should learn as much as possible, and that they should do this in the same short space of time as was required in other schools where the learning was mechanical and superficial, and where Pestalozzi's solid grounding in the elements of learning was absent."

When Pestalozzi's institution was started on French territory it was naturally filled to a great extent with French boys, and both French and German parents hoped that their children would mutually profit by the daily intercourse, so as to acquire the use of a foreign tongue.

They were far from understanding Pestalozzi's aims, and much time was frequently lost in demonstrating to them the results of the teaching.

Froebel and his pupils joined in the vigorous and active life of the school; they at once felt the charm of the lovely country surrounding their new home. The Castle of Yverdun is beautifully situated on the south side of the Lake of Neuchatel, and at the mouth of the River Orbe. From the four solid stately towers of the old Burgundian castle, built in memory of Charles the Bold, one looks across a lovely landscape. On the north-west are the high peaks of the Jura chain; on the east a vast panorama of distant mountains and glaciers. On the north-east the beautiful lake is surrounded by pine-clad hills. Before Pestalozzi and his merry company of boys took up their abode in the

Castle it was a dismal place, tenanted only by rooks and crows, and the only pleasing thing about it was the fresh green meadow-land which lay between it and the lake. Now the formerly silent and deserted rooms were filled with a powerful and stirring life.

It was Froebel's wish to live within the walls of the institution with his boys, so as to come daily under Pestalozzi's personal influence. But this was found to be impossible, and he had to content himself with a home near enough to allow them to share the lessons, walks, meals, holidays, etc., with the other pupils.

The arrangements in the Castle of Yverdun were of the simplest. The class-rooms, dormitories, and dining-hall were spacious enough, but nowhere was there any attempt at comfort or convenience. Blochmann, a well-known teacher in the institution, has described some of the shifts which the teachers had to make, such as erecting their own desks in the midst of crowded class-rooms, or partitioning off for themselves a little corner in which to teach.

But the exquisite scenery made up for a good deal; they had the green meadows for the boys to romp and play in, and the clear waters of the lake for their health and refreshment. On Saturdays they would wander, after school, into the Jura mountains, or visit the neighbouring shepherds' huts. Here, at sunset, they enjoyed the lovely panorama of the Mont Blanc range and the lakes of Geneva and Neuchatel. Or perhaps they would climb in the early morning to the highest point of the Chasseral, to see the land which Cæsar once made the starting-point for the conquest of the world. Or they would eagerly collect and discuss the variety of plants growing on these heights; and teachers and pupils would go back to the valley laden and decked with their many-coloured treasures. On festive occasions pilgrimages were made to some beautiful spot on the Lake of Geneva; sometimes they would venture as far as the Canton of Valais, in Savoy, and in the summer holidays they would even penetrate as far as Mont St. Gothard, in the Bernese Oberland. What a healthful, joyous, and exhilarating life it was! Blochmann tells us that the pupils rose at five and the teachers at four, or even earlier. The teachers, indeed, had to pledge themselves to take their turns in guarding the Castle at night-time, one taking the watch till midnight, another after midnight, each in turn waking Pestalozzi at two o'clock, and the other teachers at whatever hour they fixed upon. The pupils prepared their lessons from six to seven; then Pestalozzi conducted morning prayers. These were attended by everyone. After prayers the children washed in the courtyard, the stronger of them standing, even in winter, naked in the frozen stream. Both teachers and pupils went about with bare heads and uncovered necks.

The attendance was called immediately after breakfast, and then followed lessons on scripture, language, number and form. At noon teachers and pupils, young and old, hastened to the lake to play, bathe or swim till dinner-time. The dinner was frugal and short, and lessons began again at two o'clock. Four to five was devoted to gymnastics, recreation, and refreshment; then there was work again for three hours, after which came supper and prayers. The pupils went to bed at nine o'clock, after which the teachers attended teachers' meetings or lectures on pedagogy, or Pestalozzi would have interviews with any boys the teachers brought him as deserving of praise or remonstrance.

Froebel attended all the lessons with his pupils, and had frequent and interesting discussions on method with Pestalozzi. "Although," he says, "I was not blind to the imperfections of the school, nor to the discord and want of harmony already apparent among the teachers, I thought I could trace Pestalozzi's meaning beneath the errors in practice. I was carried away by the stirring life by which I was surrounded. What was missing in unity, clearness, and connectedness was compensated for by the vigour, enthusiasm, and the geniality that underlay the doings of the whole community. Pestalozzi's discourses had a marvellous effect, and though it was not easy for him to impart his own ideals to his hearers, he always managed to stimulate and inspire them with the love of what was noble and good."

Blochmann says that the years spent at Yverdun were filled with "valuable experiences for the teacher never to be forgotten." "The daily association with so grand a personality as Pestalozzi," says Friedrich Mann, "could not fail to have the most beneficial and lasting effect upon all those who came within his sphere of activity. He was full of rich intellectual conceptions, and still fuller of pure self-sacrificing love. One could not resist the wish to reach his lofty ideal." By the beginning of the year 1809 Froebel had learned so to identify himself with the vigorous life of the place that the disagreement of Pestalozzi's two chief assistants failed to impress him as fundamental. Intercourse with the many well-educated and even distinguished men who visited Yverdun during his stay there was an important factor in Froebel's development. The various views and convictions of such a heterogeneous company led to many interesting discussions, and brought out the strength and individuality of the different opponents. In the short summary of the Pestalozzian system sent to the Duchess of Rudolstadt, Froebel says :—

"The Pestalozzian education begins at the child's birth. The child is to be harmoniously educated as a whole from the beginning; neither his body, his mind, nor his spirit must be overlooked; Pestalozzi's object is to develop all the faculties of the human being, rather than to train certain faculties to the injury of others.

"The senses and spirit of the child are the first to mature; the dawn of a child's soul is seen in its first smile; that of his intelligence in his first clear perception of an object. This is explained in Pestalozzi's *Mother's Book*, in which he shows how the child, starting with mere sense-impressions, gradually arrives at conscious perceptions. And it is to this end that the mother attracts his attention to the various objects by which he is surrounded. Not that father, mother, or teacher, are to copy Pestalozzi's plan pedantically; his object in writing the book was merely to pattern forth a method of getting the child to recognise and appreciate the world of objects in which he finds himself.* Various exercises are suggested with a view to testing the child's understanding of language.† In this way the mother trains at one and the same time the child's faculty of speech and power of observation. He soon becomes conscious of the objects about him, and learns to recall them when absent. From the narrow circle of the home he extends his observations to the wider field of nature.

* Kruesi contributed to the *Mother's Book*.
† Froebel notes here the educational value of contrasts, so characteristic of his own work later.

"The mother's duty is to emphasise and confirm these sense-impressions by repetition, and to teach the child to discriminate between them; finally, by naming objects, to recall their images to the child's mind. Next, by learning the attributes or qualities of objects, he is enabled to compare them and know them still better. And thus he learns to converse, and becomes a social creature. The child's love of imitating sounds and movements develops him in many ways. He sees the world no longer as a chaotic mass, but as divisible into objects, having various qualities. Some qualities he finds in all objects, such as number, size, proportion. Indeed, he gets his first lessons in number and form long before there is any question of formal learning.

"When the child is seven years old the mother's teaching is succeeded by that of the father or of the teacher, and the lessons, instead of being casual and intermixed, are more definitely divided off. The child is now a pupil. His power of speech is fully developed, and he begins to understand the importance of language, and his daily observations lead him to understand it better and better.

"Suitable questions on the objects observed provide ample exercise for his power of expression, which in its turn serves to develop his thinking power. Next follow exercises in the comparison of natural objects, with a view to their discrimination, the noting of likeness and difference between them. Then the surface and products of the earth are the subjects of investigation. This gives the child a more complete and thorough knowledge of the objects already observed, of their qualities, parts, connection, and classification. The study of the earth naturally interests the child in geographical facts; these are best learned at first hand, by walks with teacher or parent, and by actual observation of the country and products around his home (Heimathskunde).

"Gradually his rambles extend, so as to cover more and more ground, and he learns the meaning of plain, hill, valley, and country, whilst his interest in the various phenomena presented to him encourages him to seek for their cause. Following upon this general study he may select, say, a river near his home, learn such facts connected with it as its length and width, position, rapidity, the direction in which it flows, its banks, bed, and tributaries. Thus mastered, this river will serve him as a type for the study of all others.

"The study of rivers leads the pupil to that of the water-system of a country, and its dependence on the mountain system, and so on to its physical and political conditions, and the course may be completed by pictures and descriptions of natural scenery. Pestalozzi's course may be indicated as follows:

"1. Description of the earth's surface (Heimath-kunde).
 (*a*) The mountain system.
 (*b*) The water system.
 (*c*) Connection of these.
 (*d*) Topography.
"2. Political geography.
 Interaction of political and physical conditions.
"3. Description of the physical features of the earth.

"Roger de Guimps says: 'Pestalozzi's method of teaching geography has completely revolutionised the teaching of that science. The child is first taught to observe the country about his home, not on the map, but on the land itself; it is the child himself who draws the map, correcting the mistakes in his first attempt after further visits to the spot. Having thus learned to understand and read maps, he continues his study by the help of large blank maps hung on the wall. From the very first day geography is connected with other sciences, such as natural history, agriculture, local geology, etc., which make it very attractive even for children.

"The study of number follows upon the mother's exercises in counting. The pupil now deals with particular numbers, compares one number with another, manipulates first simple, and then more complex numbers, and finally comes to the study of arithmetic proper. In the same way a knowledge of form is obtained. Froebel recommends for the study of this subject a work by Schmidt, whom he calls "the most genial of Pestalozzi's followers." The study of form and number leads naturally to what Pestalozzi has called "the theory of magnitudes."

"'As a contrast to these mathematical studies, which provide exercises for the intellect chiefly, there are the nature studies, which serve in great part to train the emotions and the æsthetic sense. Pre-eminent, however, among the studies that affect feeling is music, the purest and loftiest gift of expression which heaven has given to man.'"

Naegeli and Pfeiffer were at this time occupied in the compilation of a Pestalozzian singing-book for children (published in 1810).

Pfeiffer, the author of a popular method of teaching singing, was a thorough pedagogue. Naegeli, a clever musician and a man of culture, was well known throughout Germany and Switzerland as the author of an excellent method of voice training. Froebel learnt much from Naegeli's lectures on music. One point especially impressed him, *i.e.*, that singing is just as valuable a means of expression for the little child as movement or speech. Froebel made a careful study of the Pfeiffer-Naegeli method of music teaching, the influence of which may be traced in the prominence given to music teaching in the Kindergarten.

Schmidt elaborated a Pestalozzian course of drawing, reading, and writing, beginning with the child's eighth year. In reading Pestalozzi followed Krug's* phonic

* Krug, 1771 to 1843.

method, but insisted on the pupil's consciousness of the physiological mechanism of speech; the system was approved and adopted by Froebel and other teachers from Yverdun.

For writing Pestalozzi at first used chequers, but Tillich recommended the substitution of rhombs, whilst Schmidt advocated the freer movement of the hand, and indeed of the whole body, when writing.

On leaving Yverdun Froebel carried with him a deep sense of the importance and value of Pestalozzi's work, and he considered those schools fortunate in which the Pestalozzian system was carried out. The system seemed to him to satisfy the natural demands both of pupil and teacher. It gave ample scope to the teacher's power of thought and feeling, and provided a pleasing variety for the pupil. He thought the practical nature of the occupations not only developed the pupil on all sides, but greatly increased his interest in his work. Froebel indicates the following grades for Pestalozzian schools: an infant class, for which the *Mother's Book* is sufficient; a first school* class, in which lessons in form, number, reading, writing, singing, scripture, and nature are given; and a second or higher (transition) class, in which the same subjects are taught a little more formally.

It is evident that Froebel's stay at Yverdun had a most important influence on the work to which he ultimately devoted himself. It was his genuine sympathy with Pestalozzi and his views that finally turned his thought away from the school proper and set it in the direction of the earliest training of the

---

* What we should call a first transition.

child, and the preparation of the mother to undertake it. Lecturing was not enough. Mothers should see, he said, their children at work under the Pestalozzian influence. Their happiness alone would convert the mothers. And as for the children, from how much evil would such a beneficent system of early training save them. Think of the faults resulting from ennui and idleness alone! and contrast this with the happiness and cheerful industry resulting from the healthy and natural use of the faculties, and the scope for childish impulses and instincts provided by Pestalozzi! How many good-for-nothing street arabs might, by proper treatment, grow up good, trustworthy citizens, and upright and intelligent fathers and mothers!

Froebel spent a good part of his leisure time at Yverdun in the open air, enjoying its beautiful situation, the sunset glow upon the glaciers, and the impressive solemnity of the forest trees. Pestalozzi's lectures to the teachers were full of suggestions of nobility, goodness, and love of humanity. But they were often misunderstood or misinterpreted, and the sad dissensions between the master and his so-called followers was but too evident. Niederer issued a highly philosophical circular on the intuitive method, which was altogether beyond the conscious aims of Pestalozzi, who felt himself unable to explain it. He says that he allowed himself to be disturbed and confused by a "crude and immature philosophy"; by a "too hasty organisation of elementary education"; by an exaggerated pedantry that bears the stamp of "another mind than his."*

* Pestalozzi often said naïvely, "I no longer understand myself, Herr Niederer will tell you what I mean."

Under these circumstances it was not unnatural for Pestalozzi to cling more and more to the support of a strong, realistic, and thoroughly practical nature like that of Joseph Schmidt, who, for the moment, was the most important figure on the scene. This bright, energetic, and intelligent young teacher was for a time the chief support of the institution, and it was on his discretion and judgment that pupils, teachers, and friends of the institution depended. He and Niederer took opposite sides in the disputes and dissensions from which the institution was suffering; and the other teachers supported, some one, some the other. Poor Pestalozzi was not strong enough to stem the current of the strife, and his New Year's speech of 1809, in spite of the "buzzing sound of success around him, is filled with bitterness and sadness."

These disturbances at length found vent in the Swiss papers, and doubt and suspicion were expressed with regard to the system employed at Yverdun. Niederer now persuaded Pestalozzi to consent to a public examination of the school, whilst Schmidt did all he could to prevent it. The Commissioners arrived in November, and whilst commending the work done by Schmidt, they were not long in detecting the contradiction between the Pestalozzian theories as expressed in Niederer's circular and what they now saw of the practice in the institution itself. Schmidt advised a diminution in the number of pupils, and a re-organisation of the household management, but again he was opposed by the other teachers, and, unfortunately for the institution, he left it in the summer of 1810. Schmidt was Pestalozzi's favourite teacher and chief

support, and his loss was a grief and a misfortune.*
Froebel (and several other distinguished students, such
as Von Tuerk, Hofmann, and Muralt) left Yverdun
the same year (1810), explaining to Pestalozzi in his
usual straightforward, honest way, the views on education he had by this time arrived at, and his plans
for studying Natural Science, and perhaps the Classics,
at one of the Universities. Niederer's philosophical
explanation of the Pestalozzian nature teaching was
unsatisfactory to him. He knew that Pestalozzi's
starting-point had been determined rather by the
needs of the people than by the dictates of psychology,
and that Niederer, though an enthusiastic theorist, was
incapable of demonstrating in practice the truth of
what he preached. Froebel's object was to carry out
Pestalozzi's idea on a thoroughly scientific method.

He returned to Frankfurt in the autumn of 1810,
by way of Berne, Schaffhausen, and Stuttgart. But
his engagement with the Holzhausens did not terminate
till July, 1811; hence he only reached Göttingen in
the middle of the summer term, the remainder of
which he utilised in elaborating his plans for the
autumn session.

* The breaking up of the school may be attributed to the disagreements between Schmidt and Niederer (the representatives of the theory and practice of Pestalozzianism).

CHAPTER IV.

THE UNIVERSITY, THE BATTLEFIELD, THE MINERALOGICAL MUSEUM.

1811 TO 1816. GÖTTINGEN AND BERLIN.

Science Studies at Göttingen—Study of Mankind—Oriental Languages—Greek—Astronomy—Science in Germany—Berlin—Professor Weiss—Plamann and his School—Political Agitations—Froebel a Volunteer—Middendorff and Langethal—On the March—Soldier and Educator—Studies in Berlin—Reunion of the Three Friends—Education the conscious aim.

GÖTTINGEN was well chosen for Froebel's purpose. It had shown its progressiveness by its richly-endowed science schools, its excellent lectures on Natural Philosophy, and its cosmopolitan spirit, which, together with its beautiful situation, attracted many foreign students. To the literary world Göttingen was interesting on account of its associations with the brotherhood of youthful poets, who, under Klopstock, Boie, and Voss, had done homage to early Teutonic poetry and song. It was in the oak avenue at the foot of the Hainberg that, on a fine moonlight night of 1772, these young enthusiasts had met to swear fealty to friendship, poetry, and virtue. Hither also had come the genial brothers Humboldt.*

* Alexander von Humboldt (1769 to 1858) came to Göttingen to study under Blumenbach, who was at Göttingen from 1778 till 1835. His lectures were more numerously attended than those of any other professor. Indeed he was so well known that a letter from America, addressed "Blumenbach, Europe," found him. Humboldt afterwards became a pupil of the eminent geologist Von Werner.

Froebel hoped here to satisfy his longing for knowledge. He too, like Alexander von Humboldt, had started with the faculty of Finance and then gone over to Natural Philosophy, which, however, in Froebel's case was to serve as the basis for the study of man.

Froebel's knowledge of himself and of life had made great strides during the nine years which had elapsed since his visit to Jena. He was now clearly conscious that his ultimate object was to find *a scientific way of educating the human being.* He felt deeply the want of the self-development and culture necessary for a right understanding of scientific method. His first duty, therefore, was to select from the curriculum pursued at Göttingen such subjects as would enable him to lay a basis of education in harmony with the nature of man. It happened, fortunately for Froebel, that the scientific investigations of his time ran in two directions which were both practical for his purpose and congenial to his tastes, *i.e.*, Natural Science and the origin of language.* Hence, in addition to several branches of science, he began to study the development of language, from man's first utterances to our own day. Froebel had a large intellectual appetite, and he plunged undismayed into the study of the Indian, Persian and Hebrew languages, Latin, Greek, and Philology. It was from the point of view of the natural science of mind that language interested him; and perceiving that language had developed in the race slowly and gradually, he determined to follow this course himself, feeling, like

---

* "Language," says Humboldt, "is the most delicate blossom of the mind."—*Kosmos.*

Herbart, that the individual must go through the experience of the race. He worked through the summer term with the utmost energy, but the immensity of the subject, and his desire for thoroughness, did but impress upon him his unpreparedness. The text-books at hand seemed to him superficial and artificial, and in no way calculated to develop a scientific knowledge of language.* Sylvestre de Sacy's *Arabic Grammar* was not published till 1810, and it was not till somewhere about 1820 that German scholars took up the study of Oriental languages seriously. After a good deal of persistent but vain effort to gain what he wanted from existing Hebrew and Arabic text-books, Froebel at length yielded to the opinion of those more experienced than himself, who declared that from a pedagogic point of view he was losing time. After this his language study was limited for some time to Greek, the regularity of which had a great fascination for him.

In the evenings he would seek rest and refreshment in the beautiful woods around Göttingen, and often stayed out on the Hainberg till midnight watching the stars. This pursuit so keenly interested him that he would frequently rise in the night to make notes of his observations. It was at this time that Froebel began to look upon the sphere as the typical curved form (all others being but modifications of this). The sphere symbolised to him both infinite development and limitation—variety in unity, unity in variety; connectedness in all things; what Leibnitz called

* The best books on the subject had only recently been published, e.g., Herder's *Spirit of Hebrew Poetry* (1783); Salomo's *Songs of Love* (1778); a German edition of *Sakontala*, by the Indian poet Kalidasa (1803); and finally Schlegel's *Wisdom of the Indians* (1808).

"harmony of body and soul." It formed a bond between the complete and the incomplete; the macrocosm and microcosm. Further, it exemplified as no other form did, the threefold principle underlying the education of man, *i.e., unity*, or completeness; *variety*, or all-sidedness; and *individuality*, or that which marks the highest development in man. The sphere seemed to him the embodiment of a principle equally applicable to the development of man and nature, and to indicate the starting-point for the education of the child. At the same time he had come to the conclusion that it was in natural science that the keystone to the education of man would be found, and that henceforth that was his main subject, language and mathematics being but subservient to it. To add to Froebel's interest in nature there appeared this year (1811) the famous comet, one of the most beautiful that had ever been seen. Like the Sicilian comet of 1807, this one showed, in Herschel's large telescope, a well-defined disk. The intensity of light at the centre was greater than had ever been seen; and the mist around it was separated from the sweeping curve of the tail by a dark space. The tail was calculated by astronomers to be one hundred million miles long, and the diameter of the disk eighty times that of the earth, and seven times that of Jupiter, whilst the period it occupied to pass through its entire orbit was 3065 years. It had been predicted that this comet would bring misfortune.*

* Alexander von Humboldt says:—"It lies in the somewhat sad and serious nature of men to regard the unexpected rather with fear than with hope or joy. The wonder of a great comet, suddenly appearing in the heavens, with its cloudy mantle, is everywhere felt as something hostile; as an attack upon the established order of things."

The prophecy appeared to be justified by the political events in Europe at the time.

Froebel spent the summer holiday very happily in the united and industrious family of his brother Christian, at Osterode, in the Harz Mountains. He interested himself in the children's education, and in his brother's business.*

On his return to Göttingen he worked hard at natural history, biology, and mineralogy. He followed with great interest the recent impetus given to scientific research in Europe.†

Scientific discovery was a good deal hindered in Germany by the prevalence of Kant's speculative and critical method. It was only by dint of slow and patient effort that Alexander von Humboldt succeeded in introducing the inductive method of reasoning.

Froebel, to a certain extent, was safeguarded from

---

* Christian Froebel had a weaving factory.

† In France, Lavoisier (1728-1799) had already been guillotined, but not before he had done much to introduce quantitative methods into chemistry. In England, Black (1728-1799), Cavendish (1731-1810), and Priestley (1735-1804) had made researches in chemistry and physics, and had investigated gases. In Sweden, Bergmann (1743-1786) had discovered and investigated many substances. The above all believed in the phlogiston theory, or some modification of it. According to this theory all combustible bodies contained a certain principle "phlogiston," which they gave up when burnt. This theory was now being replaced by the atomic theory, the principal advocate of which was John Dalton (1766-1844), and the theory of oxidation. Gay Lussac (1778-1850) and Davy (1778-1829) were inquiring into electricity and chemistry and their mutual relationship. These, with Vauquelin (1763-1829) and others, devised new methods of chemical analysis, and continued the investigations of their predecessors into the nature of various gaseous substances. Chemistry was advancing to the position of an exact science, and was beginning to be applied usefully to manufactures and agriculture.—Note by Mr. A. MARSHALL.

the mystic philosophy of his time by his tendency to practical investigation, but it was impossible for him to remain altogether unaffected by it. The various branches of study he entered upon at Göttingen, *i.e.*, chemistry, biology, natural history, political economy, and the like, were all subservient to his one great aim, *i.e.*, to find one law applicable to the organic and inorganic, to man and nature. From chemistry he naturally proceeded to the study of mineralogy, and his interest in crystals became so absorbing that he determined to go to the University of Berlin to work under the great Professor Weiss (1710 to 1856), von Werner's most renowned pupil. This decision was strengthened not only by the fact that he was dissatisfied with the teaching of this subject at Göttingen, but also that in Berlin he would have more opportunity of earning the fees for further study. He left Göttingen in the summer of 1812, and settled in Berlin.

The Berlin University, though but three years old, was already renowned. Its founders* hoped to make it the centre of German scientific culture and advanced thought. Thus, in the very heart of the gay, pretentious, political and official Berlin, there was a stirring and powerful intellectual life. Weiss had developed the mathematical side of mineralogy to a high degree, and had given mathematical names to the facets of crystals, according to the position and inter-relationship of their axes and zones.†

He was familiar with the most recent discoveries

---

* These were Wilhelm von Humboldt, Fichte, Schleiermacher, Savigny, Niebuhr, Marheinecke, Weiss, and others.
† See WEISS' *Natural Classification of Crystals*, published in 1813.

in chemistry, and his simple and natural system was one after Froebel's own heart, and served further to confirm his idea of cosmic evolution and unity in nature.

It was not surprising that the new interest in natural phenomena should lead to a revolt from artificial and conventional modes of education. The old routine had already sustained a serious shock by the publication of Rousseau's *Emile*, which was but the expression of principles that had been gradually forming themselves in Europe for several centuries. Amongst the most distinguished advocates of these principles were Basedow, Campe,* Gedike and Rochow.† The time had now come for tackling the error that a mind can be educated by imposing upon it ready-made ideas. The keynote of the new educa-

* Joachim Heinrich Campe (1746-1818) is known as one of Basedow's associates for a time in the famous Philanthropinum at Dessau; as the founder of a similar educational institute near Hamburg; as a writer of books for children, and publisher of German translations of certain notable pedagogical works, such as Locke's *Thoughts on Education*, and Rousseau's *Emile*.

† Friedrich Eberhard von Rochow (1734-1805), after some experiences of military life, settled on his estate near Brandenburg, and devoted himself to the benefit of his people. In the years 1771 to 1772, when famine and disease spread far and wide, he engaged a regular physician for the peasants on his estate; but the people, ignorant and prejudiced, would not use the medicines provided for them, and secretly applied to quacks and miracle doctors; in consequence many died a miserable death. The disastrous results of ignorance impressed the philanthropist. He saw that the social reforms he desired were impossible apart from the cultivation of the people's intelligence by better education. To provide a better education became the immediate object of his life. With this object in view he wrote books which circulated far and wide (*The Kinderfreund*, etc.), and carrying out reforms in certain schools over which he had power, imparted the first impulse to the reformation of the popular schools in Saxony.—Note by K. M. CLARKE.

tion was Bacon's saying that "Nihil est in intellectu quod non fuerit in sensu"—"A thinking being is the sum of his senses."

Actual objects had come to be considered as a necessary means of education. Comenius had, it is true, long ago raised his voice in protest against abstract teaching, but men's minds were at the time too much occupied with the disturbances consequent upon the Thirty Years War (1618 to 1648) for him to gain a hearing; and Pestalozzi had probably not heard the name of Comenius when he enunciated his principle that "Observation is the beginning, and understanding the end of education." Froebel adopted the Pestalozzian principle of Anschauung as the basis of his system, and thus continued the stream of educational progress already started. At the same time his practical application of the principle was a new departure; and his insistence on continuity introduced a harmony and order into education, similar to that introduced by Alexander von Humboldt into science by the discovery of the stone (which had hitherto been regarded as an inert mass of material) as a living link in the chain of evolution.

Soon after his arrival in Berlin, Froebel was fortunate enough to obtain a post as teacher in a higher grade Pestalozzian school then under Johann Ernst Plamann (1771 to 1834). This relieved him of any anxiety about money matters. Plamann was the most distinguished of Pestalozzi's immediate followers; and to judge from the criticisms of his contemporaries, he carried out Pestalozzi's educational ideas better than did those teachers who were under his own direction. He himself possessed considerable scientific culture, and his psychological insight enabled him to gauge the nobility and purity of Pestalozzi's character and aims. And though he could see that these aims were but imperfectly carried out at Burgdorf, where, in 1803, he had made the master's acquaintance, he felt that the Swiss pedagogue had the true view of education. Plamann's special work was the adaptation of the Pestalozzian system to higher grade schools. To this end, in 1805, amidst great difficulties, he succeeded in starting a school on the new method, and published Pestalozzi's *Fundamental Principles of Instruction applied to the Teaching of Natural History, Geography, and Language.* Pestalozzi, who had evolved his system from experience rather than from abstract reasoning, much appreciated Plamann's philosophical conception of it, and his skilful adaptation of the Pestalozzian principles to instruction generally.*

To Froebel the school offered little that was new; its popularity and success, like that of the institution at Yverdun, had its disadvantages; successful schools are seldom free from interested aims. Here, too, Froebel missed the unity of plan and the higher motive power he looked for. What he wanted to see was a better understanding of the nature of the human being, and especially of the child. He undertook no responsibility in the general management of the school, and so came little under its general tone. The time not occupied in preparing his own lessons was devoted

---

* The affection between Plamann and Pestalozzi was that of father and son. "At his side," says Plamann, "I learned my own ignorance and acknowledged it tearfully." Pestalozzi replied, 'You have a great advantage over me, in having had the discipline of a scientific training.' And he was moved to tears at a little poem I had written on him, and said, 'You understand me better than anyone.'"

to academical studies. He was much interested in Professor Jahn,* Principal of a Drilling and Fencing School. This school formed the nucleus of a group of enthusiastic young Prussian patriots, who banded themselves together to promote manliness and virtue. These young patriots responded warmly to the king's appeal to "my people," and joined the German Confederation, sharing in the general excitement caused by Napoleon's campaigns, and the European alliance formed against him. Hatred of the foreign yoke, and a zeal for national freedom, was the cry of people of all ages and of every class. Students and teachers left their lectures and their schools, labourers and artisans their workshops, and peasants their ploughs, to fight for their country.

All Berlin was roused, and Froebel did not escape the general stir and movement, though, as he says, "being no Prussian, and living a very quiet, studious life, Fichte's appeal did not mean so much to me as to others. I determined," he says, "rather with firmness than with enthusiasm, to join the volunteers; I was an enthusiast for the development of a national spirit; I was a German, and I wished to follow my profession in a noble way. Moreover, I must teach every boy to be willing to defend his country; and how could I, a young fellow capable of taking arms, undertake to train boys as patriots, unless I was willing to set them the example? Would they not despise me if I refused to do what I urged upon

* Friedrich Ludwig Jahn (1778 to 1852) was an earnest advocate of physical training as a means of national regeneration. The establishment of the Turnvereins was to a great extent an outcome of the wide-spread interest in physical exercise he aroused. A monument in his honour was erected in Berlin in 1872.

them? And did not this appeal to the nation express a crying need of the country, and the time in which I lived? and would it not be unworthy and unmanly to refuse to share in the common danger? Such were the thoughts that overcame my natural disinclination and my physical unfitness for a soldier's life."

Such was the spirit in which he, with Jahn and seven other young patriots, marched to Breslau, in 1813. Here they enrolled themselves in Lützow's corps of black riflemen. The poet Koerner was one of this company.*

They formed part of the infantry division, whose chief duty consisted in raising recruits, and carrying on predatory operations in the rear of the enemy. With these they marched to Dresden. Neither in Dresden nor elsewhere during the campaign did Froebel make many acquaintances. But two most remarkable friendships were the result of his short military career. Jahn's little battalion had been ordered to march to Leipzig. At their first halt Froebel was introduced by Jahn to a young Thuringian, named Heinrich Langethal. Langethal introduced to Froebel his great friend Wilhelm Middendorff, and from this moment a trio of friendship was formed which banded together three noble hearts in the most

---

* Theodor Koerner (1791 to 1813) was a patriotic poet who served and fell in the War of Liberation. The following verses refer to Lützow's "Wilde Jagd," the corps in which the author and Froebel were fellow volunteers:—

"See there in the valley they rush in the fight,
 Where sabres and helmets are clashing;
 From their blades, as on helmets of steel they smite,
 Through the smoke of the battle there glistens a light,
 The sparks of our freedom are flashing.
 What mean the black horsemen who ride such a race?
 That is Lützow's fearless and desperate chase."

—Note by K. M. CLARKE.

self-sacrificing effort for the good of mankind. They were all fired by enthusiasm, and as they sang their patriotic songs, they pledged each other in the wine of the country, amidst clinking of glasses, as is the German custom. They found much to say to each other. The mild evening air on the banks of the Elbe, the restfulness and peace after the day's march, the intense interest awakened in the minds of the two younger men by Froebel's views on patriotism and education,—all combined to prolong their discussions till late in the night. Henceforth the two young men were Froebel's devoted friends and disciples, one might almost say, leaving all to " cling only unto him." Middendorff's ideas of friendship were intensified by an exceedingly poetic temperament, and Froebel's educational idea seemed from the first moment to take entire possession of him. The friends shared the same rooms, and many were the discussions they had together on military service, human life, and the new scheme of education.

Heinrich Langethal was born at Erfurt in 1792, Middendorff near Dortmund in 1793, so they were Froebel's juniors by ten years. "Father Jahn" had described Froebel as a "queer creature, who made fairy tales out of stones and cobwebs." They were both what is called students of philosophy, and disciples of Fichte, Schleiermacher,* and Neander.†

* Friedrich Ernst Schleiermacher (1768 to 1834) opposed in certain important respects orthodox Lutheran doctrines, and attempted in *The Christian Faith* to elaborate "a new evangelical theology." He taught that religion is personal, subjective—a consciousness in the individual soul of dependence upon God, and communion with God. De Wette was a disciple of Schleiermacher, who did work of some importance in Biblical criticism.—K. M. CLARKE.

† Neander, born 1789, of Jewish race, was the author of a great work on ecclesiastical history ; a work characterized by its liberality of thought.—K. M. CLARKE.

The three friends fought side by side at the battles of Gross-Goerschen,* Luetzen, and Goehrde. During an armistice (proclaimed on June 7th) their battalion was quartered at Havelberg, and drilled daily. Froebel did not object to the coercion of the drill. On the contrary, he was much interested in the promptness, decision, and general moral discipline it developed. He enjoyed the marching through the bright spring air, and his interest in nature never flagged. He neglected no opportunity of observing the laws of development in the plants and other objects that came in his way. The beautiful surroundings of Havelberg were a source of great enjoyment to him. He read Forster's *Rhine Land*, a favourite book of Alexander von Humboldt, during the campaign.

His short military service provided our philosopher with much food for reflection, on the solidarity of the human race; the destiny of the human being; and the interaction of mind and body. The war itself was but a dream to him, as he was generally far from the scene of action, and, much to his regret, seldom understood the orders he had to follow. But in spite of this discouragement, he never lost the enthusiasm for the welfare of his country which Fichte had awakened within him, and "everywhere," he says, "my future mission was present to my mind." The corps was dismissed after the Peace of Paris (31st May, 1814), and Froebel proceeded by way of Düsseldorf, Mainz, Frankfurt, and Rudolstadt, to Berlin, where he obtained the post (promised him by Professor Weiss at the beginning of the war) of Curator of the Mineralogical Museum. By the month of August he found himself

* Scharnhorst was fatally wounded in this battle.

at work in the silent and secluded rooms devoted to the mineralogical collection, and began to arrange and classify the specimens before him, verifying at each step the unity of plan in geology which the poet Goethe was occupied in tracing throughout the vegetable world. "I read here more clearly than ever," he says, "the divine in small as well as in great things. The smallest crystal form serves as a mirror of human development." Thus a flood of light was shed upon his nature studies; nature and man explained each other; and he realised more and more the value of an early and an intimate acquaintance with nature's laws and processes. Only so would science and education mutually assist each other. His lectures at the Berlin University helped him little. Much more to the purpose were his investigations amongst his crystals and other natural objects, and his observations in astronomy, and even in human speech.* Froebel's object in tracing the law of evolution in these various directions was to find a scientific basis for the education of man.

His idea at this time was to prepare himself for teaching either in a higher grade school or at the University. But he felt that a scientific training was, after all, of less real importance for him than a knowledge of the human being. The education and development of the human being in a "natural and harmonious" way; the fitting him to respond to nature's demands upon him at every stage of his development: this was the task he was gradually learning to set before himself. Nature was his type,

* Froebel had a theory which explained the vowel sounds in a language to be its spirit and strength, each vowel having its special function, and the consonants its clothing or flesh.

and "if man," he says, "is ever to fulfil his destiny, and to avoid the errors that prevent him reaching the goal, he must, from the very first and throughout, be trained in accordance with the laws of development."

Langethal and Middendorff, hoping for promotion, had remained with the army till Napoleon's escape from Elba (1815), when such a rush of German youths presented themselves as volunteers, that a Royal proclamation was issued, forbidding Government officials and University students to serve. The two young men thus returned to their studies, and soon found work in Berlin as private tutors. They brought their difficulties to Froebel, who gave them, twice a week, instruction in mathematics. Middendorff, who intended to stay but a short time in Berlin, shared Froebel's lodging, and the two friends became deeply attached to one another.

The association with these earnest young friends, who showed such confidence in his more mature experience and riper judgment, further inspired our mineralogist with thoughts about education, and he soon became so absorbed with the subject that he refused at this time a professorship of mineralogy in Stockholm, determining to sacrifice everything for what he regarded as his mission. His recent studies had suggested to him a principle which he longed to apply to education, and which he published many years later (*i.e.*, in 1840) as the law of the conciliation of contrasts, or the law of the spherical, which symbolizes all development.*

---

* *i.e.*, activity in three directions, towards (1) unity, (2) variety, (3) individuality. See A. B. HANSCHMANN's pamphlet on the *Kindergarten System* (published 1874).

Here, at length, was the solution to the problem of human development. Only by means of this threefold activity would man be enabled to express his true being and essence. Only so would he practically prove himself to be one of nature's products. Man's nature required that he should express himself in these three directions, *i.e.*, as a complete whole; as variously gifted; as true to himself. Only an education worthy the name would assist him to this. Having arrived at this conclusion Froebel longed to test the principle, and determined, much to the regret of his employers, to leave Berlin. This he did in October, 1816, and for some time his two friends heard nothing of him. They had to content themselves with his promise that as soon as things were ripe for action he would let them know.

CHAPTER V.

FROEBEL'S SCHOOL FOR BOYS.

1816 TO 1826. GRIESHEIM AND KEILHAU.

Froebel's First School at Griesheim—Learning by Doing—Arrival of Middendorff, the Life-long Friend and Ally—His Sympathy with the Boys—Tone of the School—Privations—Training in Patriotism —School Building—Froebel's Main Principles—Plans and Hopes —Difficulties—Middendorff's Love of Nature—Natural Education —Arrival of Langethal—His Influence on the Boys—Correct Speaking—Training in Endurance—Testimony of Pupils— Froebel's Pestalozzianism—Logical Exercises—Language Teaching —Christmas, 1817—Froebel's Marriage—Changes in the School— Frau Froebel's Influence—Christmas, 1819—Gymnastics—The Luthers—Timely Aid of Brother Christian—Growth of the School —Barop—Height of Prosperity—Betrothals—Karl Froebel— Report on the School.

JUST as Froebel was about to recommence his scientific labours in Berlin, he received the sad news of his brother Christoph's death. Ever since the battle of Leipzig (1813) typhus fever had raged more or less throughout Central Germany, and it was whilst performing his pastoral duty of ministering to the sick that Christoph took the fever and died, leaving a young widow and four children—a little girl and three boys —Julius, Karl, and Theodor. It had been their father's wish that the boys should take up science, and their mother was now greatly perplexed, being well aware that the two eldest at least required better teaching than was provided by the village school. She had had many proofs of her husband's confidence in Friedrich's educational views, and naturally turned to her brother-in-law for counsel and advice. Friedrich, on his side, feeling his nephews to be a sacred trust, looked upon this as a call from heaven, and felt that his hour had come. He immediately started for Griesheim, making most of the journey on foot. He had had very little money to start with, but felt quite cheerful when, on reaching Erfurt, on the last day of his journey, he found he could only indulge in a penny loaf before tramping the last three miles. He lost all sense of fatigue as he thought of the new educational epoch he was about to inaugurate; for he had quite determined to start a school in which the training should be based on psychology and scientific pedagogy.

Late in the evening the tired wanderer arrived at the house of his sister-in-law. His nephews stared wonderingly at the long-haired man with the big, flapping hat. Froebel did all he could to comfort his sister-in-law, and promised, as far as he was able, to supply the father's place to the boys.*

During the few weeks spent at Griesheim he became greatly attached to the children, who knew how to appreciate the liberty he allowed them. They wished their uncle would live with them always. The mother and aunt of Frau Christoph, who formed part of the family, were, on the other hand, somewhat scandalised at what they looked upon as laxity of discipline and licence.

Froebel next visited his brother Christian, at Osterode, whose boys, Ferdinand and Wilhelm, he knew to be also

* It seems that Frau Christoph Froebel read a deeper meaning in this promise than was intended.

in need of a good education. Brother Christian was easily persuaded to entrust them to their uncle Friedrich, and it only remained for Froebel to find quarters in which to house the boys. A house and garden at Griesheim, not far from his sister-in-law's, was fixed upon. Griesheim is a small village on the Ilm, looking towards Ilmenau, having a view of church and castle on a neighbouring height. The village, surrounded by orchards and consisting chiefly of pasture land, lies in an open valley. Here, on the 13th November, 1816, within sight of the church of Stadt Ilm, in which his uncle Hoffmann used to preach, without means, but impelled by an inner necessity, he started on his educational scheme. Full of faith and hope, he wrote at once to beg his friends Middendorff and Langethal to join him. Nine years before, in a letter to brother Christoph, he had said, "My plan is extremely simple; what I want is a happy family school, and a peaceful life with nature around me." Here at length was the longed-for opportunity of realising his ideal. These boys should be trained in accordance with boy nature. All his teaching should be based on the self-activity of the children; they should learn by living and know by doing. Their observations, perceptions, and conclusions should be their own. Everything should start in action, movement, manipulation, and production. Life, action, and knowledge should go hand in hand. In cheerfulness, simplicity, and freedom the boys should be taught how to teach themselves. Only after having fully stimulated them to self-activity would he come to their help, and then only with a view to further stimulation. In the winter he helped them make an immense snowball, which was then rolled down an incline. This served as a starting-point for lessons on the Alps and avalanches. In the spring-time the boys took their nature lessons in field and forest, Uncle Friedrich sharing their investigations of plant and insect.

At Easter (1817) Middendorff, having completed his theological studies, was ready to join Froebel; but he had to go to Brechten, in Westphalia, in order to break the news of his determination to his parents. He had four sisters, but was the only boy, the youngest and the favourite of the family; and the one great wish of his parents had been to see him pastor in his native place. Had it not been for his utter belief in Froebel's genius, he would never have been able to resist his parents' entreaties, nor to listen unmoved to his father's parting words of submission, "We have been richly blessed. One must be offered up as a sacrifice." Middendorff arrived at Griesheim on a beautiful spring day (the 14th April, 1817), a few days before Froebel's thirty-fifth birthday, bringing with him as pupil Langethal's young brother Christian, a boy of eleven.

From this time to the end of his life Middendorff devoted himself to the service of Froebel and his idea.

His inner life was not unlike Froebel's. As a child he had been reflective and introspective. He, too, had had "glimpses of unity in life and harmony in the natural world." His son-in-law, Wichard Lange, shows how the later development of this highly gifted man consisted greatly in his gradually awakening consciousness and understanding of these early intuitions.[*] Middendorff shared Froebel's intense love of nature. "Whoever has rambled with Middendorff through field and forest," says Lange, "will be able to recall the

[*] *Jahrbuch für Lehrer und Schulfreunde*, 1855.

delight with which the unity and harmony of nature inspired him, and how he infected others with his joy in the throbbing life around, and with his eloquence over the divine goodness, beauty, and wisdom manifested in nature." Froebel's attitude towards nature was perhaps rather that of a scientist and investigator, whilst Middendorff's approached nearer to that of the poet or artist. Middendorff possessed the gift of eloquence which was lacking to Froebel. They were united in their aims and objects, and in their innocence of anything like worldly ambition; and their characteristic differences only served to unite them the more closely, by making each serve as the complement of the other.

Middendorff was at first more like a companion and friend to the boys than a teacher, his first object being to study and understand Froebel's idea. He shared the children's rambles, and entered into animated discussions with them about anything that interested them. His gentleness and kindness won all hearts. He was greatly interested in folk-lore, and delighted to hear Julius Froebel relate the saga of the origin of Griesheim and Hammersfeld; how there were two giants fighting against each other, and how one hurled a great rock from the top of the Singerberg, which stopped, however, when it got to Gries in the Ilm, and how that was the foundation of Griesheim. How the other giant threw a hammer at his enemy from the top of the Willinger-berg that stuck in a field, and gave the name to the village of Hammersfeld. Middendorff loved to stimulate the children's imagination, whilst Froebel sought rather to develop their reason and intelligence.

The boys made themselves little gardens, in which they planted such flowers as they found on the hills— purple martagon, orchids, lilies of the valley, and the magnificent *Centaures montana*. Froebel's birthday (21st April) was kept as a holiday. Teachers and children made an excursion in the Thuringian Hills, "which, in the glorious spring of that year," says Karl Froebel, "were covered with flowers." On this occasion Langethal's brother related his experiences in the recent campaign. Froebel's delight in the grandeur of the scenery, and his pleasure at the discovery of any rare plant or other natural object, opened the boys' eyes to beauties they had never seen before. Boys and teachers returned home laden with cherry-blossom and violet anemones, and made a happy party round the prettily-decorated table. Uncle Friedrich and his guests kept up an animated conversation, and when the time came for the Griesheim boys to go home* they were loth to leave so merry a company.

As Froebel's object was to develop the individuality of his pupils, they enjoyed great freedom in small matters, and the elder ladies of the family were not a little shocked to meet the boys running about bareheaded, playing in the road with mud and stones, or wading barefoot in the water. But in spite of all this the hours of the day were well and profitably filled with work, and Karl Froebel says: "From all that we did, even from our games, I seemed to be learning just what I wanted to know. We had exercises and games with the bow and arrow, spear, skipping-rope, and much besides. Indoors we were occupied with cardboard

---

* They still lived with their mother.

work, paper-weaving, perforating, drawing, etc. The lessons that most delighted me were those on form, number, proportion, and language. We all loved, too, the drawing on chequers. Froebel's teaching was a revelation to us of a new world of order, regularity, and beauty. He soon corrected our mispronunciation, and taught us to be ashamed of the rough, incorrect, or profane expressions we had learned from the village boys. He made us use real German words instead of the Germanized-French ones which had been introduced into Thuringia by the French wars, and which we only half understood."

Froebel taught the boys to choose their words carefully, and to avoid expressions that meant nothing to them, or that were likely to convey a wrong idea. The mornings were devoted to study, the afternoons to manual occupations.

On the death of her father, Frau Christoph Froebel had to give up her home at Griesheim. She took a small farm at Keilhau, about four miles away. This little village, lying amongst the quiet woods and hills of the Schaalbach Valley, was an ideal place for Froebel's work. Some rare plants and animals were to be found amongst its rocks and hills. Pine trees and laurels grew at different heights. Foxes, owls, and deer were to be met with in the neighbouring Schutzthal. Wild pigeons, thrushes, and squirrels hopped about in the pine woods, whilst the kingfisher hid on the banks of the streams. The white-throat finch, titmouse, wood-lark, and other singing birds abounded in the hedges and gardens. On the Kirschberg grew the wild lily, ascension flower (blue and white), orchid, and iris. Here was indeed an educational field for the boys. Froebel and his sister-in-law decided upon a combined household.

The village of Keilhau was quaint and curious; it consisted of a score of small cottages and farms; some of the houses were two or three hundred years old. The church, though it had a charming old tower, was like a cellar. In the main street of the village was a pool, and the roads were always moist and not unfrequently overrun by lizards and salamanders. The habits and customs of the peasants were those of the middle ages. The magistrate counted on a notched stick the fees which one or another of his neighbours had to pay as tithe or ground-rent. He also communicated verbally to the peasants any new enactment of the Government; and to complete the mediæval picture, the watchman marched daily through the village armed with a battle-axe. On Sundays the whole community assembled in the church in gala dress, but the same blue cloth coat that had been worn by the youth still adorned the old man, and the heavy blue cloth mantles of the women, with their gold tassels, were handed down from mother to daughter. Their chief food was corn and fruit, and the clear water that sparkled in the basin of the village fountain their drink. Only on occasions such as the market-day at Rudolstadt would the peasant indulge in such a luxury as a glass of beer, a herring, or maybe his favourite dish of German sausage.

Amidst this primitive life Froebel now hoped to put into practice his long-cherished scheme.

He had obtained permission to build a school-house on the widow's farm land, and had made the plans himself.

The building was started in November. Boys and teachers all helped with a right good will to lay floors, fix stoves, or level the roads round the farm, and had some valuable training for hand and eye in the process.

On the whole a gloriously happy childhood was passed in the Keilhau institution. The recent emancipation of Germany had an exhilarating effect on the teachers, who, far from regarding themselves as mere instructors of the boys, looked thoroughly after their physical health and happiness, sharing their games, swimming, fencing, and other outdoor exercises. The children looked upon Middendorff as their legitimate playmate, and the whole circle formed a happy family. At the same time there was perfect submission to the rules of the school, and Uncle Friedrich's word was law. The boys loved to hear their teachers relate their experiences in the recent campaign, or discuss questions of importance for the welfare of Germany. The history lessons served as the basis of many a small drama, in which the boys would personate the knights and heroes of the middle ages. The rivers, rocks, castles, valleys, clefts, mountain-peaks, and other striking features of the neighbourhood served as background for these imaginative plays, and were re-christened with names borrowed from feudal times. The little troop, with their long hair hanging over their gymnastic costumes or quaint little jackets, lived in a land of poetry, chivalry, asceticism, and daring.

Froebel had gone through much during the ten years that had elapsed since his first experience in teaching at Frankfurt. The contradiction between his ideal world and the reality had ceased to trouble him since he had become conscious of his mission as conciliator of this contradiction.* His progress had been from an instinctive, almost blind, effort at true development towards a conscious and independent application of the Pestalozzian principles. The feeling that Pestalozzi had not said the last word on the science of pedagogy had sent him first to Göttingen and then to Berlin. Here he had made a careful study of the works of Basedow, Comenius, Rousseau, Pestalozzi, etc. Finally Fichte's *National Education* had given him a fresh impetus, and widened his thought; for whereas before he had chiefly considered the human being as an individual, Fichte opened his eyes to the importance of training him to be part of a community. Pestalozzi, who had to supply the place of parents to the orphan children under his care, was more and more impressed with the value of home education; Fichte, on the other hand, in his enthusiasm for the education of citizens, would have robbed them of this benefit. "Do you desire a better future?" he said: "it may come, but it will not come from without, neither can the present generation bring it forth, but our children can. Thus it behoves you fathers and mothers to tear them from your hearts, and from the apathy and indifference that reigns in your minds. Hand them over to the State, or to special right-minded men, that they may not be dullards or parrots, but may be educated intelligently and have an understanding of things. Let them be trained to be men." Froebel saw the good in both views. He saw that the child who at first appears to belong exclusively to the family,

---

* See BENFEY's *Kindergarten und Elementar-Klasse.* 1860.

must of necessity widen his circle as he grows older, and pass from the limited sphere by which his mother's care surrounds him to the larger freedom and air of the outer world of humanity and nature. He will by-and-bye require the influence of other children, other human beings, and other conditions, than those of his home.

But Froebel's object was very different from Fichte's; he wanted the child to become a good citizen, but above all a complete and perfect human being, and he did not think the way to bring this about was to hand him over to the State. What he would have preferred was to see families combine together to give children the united influence of home and school. The object of his work at Keilhau was to bring about an all-round, harmonious development, in contradistinction to the one-sided education so common in his day, and for which he maintained the penalty must sooner or later be paid. The doctrines he urged on his fellow-workers, Langethal and Middendorf, were:—1st, a careful study of each individual pupil; 2nd, a skilful stimulation of his self-activity; 3rd, and above all, sympathy with childhood.

It was Froebel's intention at this time to limit the number of his pupils to twenty-four. For this number the school building had been planned, and the three teachers would have sufficed. Had Froebel kept within these limits he would have escaped many of the troubles and difficulties from which, for some years, Keilhau had to suffer. Meanwhile he threw himself heart and soul into the stream of young life by which he was surrounded. He firmly believed his mission to be the ennobling of mankind. His faith in his fellow-men led him to believe that his work would in time be recognised and appreciated. In this sanguine spirit he pursued his educational schemes, and superintended the erection of the school building and the repairing of the farm. A new building had already been begun and relinquished by the former owner of the property. There was a roof and one completed room on the ground floor, but no windows, doors, or floors, whilst the farm-house was in such a dilapidated condition as to be unfit for habitation. Froebel's plan was to turn the old house into a shed, and build the school on the site of the former shed; and, meanwhile, to rent for himself, Middendorff, and the Osterode children, the upper part of a farm-house. But even here he had to provide doors, windows, and floors, and to repair the staircase. All this fully occupied him throughout the summer months, so that he could take no part in the teaching.

Middendorff took this opportunity of rambling through the Keilhau valley with the boys. There was a splendid view from the Steiger. The road leads through a pine thicket, emerging from which the traveller suddenly sees, spread out before him, at the depth of one thousand feet, the valley of the Rinne. Facing him is the valley of the Saal, with the Castle of Weissenburg, and no less than four towns can be seen from where he stands. Middendorff interested the children in the neighbourhood by all sorts of legends and stories connected with it, *e.g.*, how once upon a time a great oak forest covered the whole district, from which the village of Eichfeld took its name, then part of the forest was cleared away, and this gave rise to the village of Lichtstaedt, which means clearing. The name of the village Schaala came from the cups or shells of the acorns which were sold there for turf; and Keilhau was so called because the first inhabitants used *Keilen* (hatchets) to hew down the strong trunks of the oak trees. Whether these names are due to Middendorff's imagination or not is uncertain. In any case he and the boys went on many a voyage of discovery together. They followed up every mountain stream to its source, and, to the great astonishment of the inhabitants, re-christened them all, *e.g.*, the Remader was now the Silberbach; the Schutzthalquelle, Mosbach; and the Steigerquelle, Schaalbach; the Scherbe, at Eichfeld, was called Schirme. Only the Pörz kept its original name, being close to the Pörz mill.

Next came the hills: they changed the Kolm into Kolben; the Steinberg into Uhuberg; and even the names of the farmers and labourers underwent similar alteration; (Ziener became Zäuner; Hänold became Hainhold) and this in spite of the protestations of the peasants themselves, who referred the innovators to the authority of their fathers, grandfathers, and great-grandfathers. But the new names having been traced to their origin by Middendorff and Froebel, and found to be correct, resistance was useless. The boys rejoiced in the discovery of various delicious wild fruits growing on the hills. They had no set lessons at this time, but they learned much in an informal way. They collected, pressed, and named all the flowers of the neighbourhood, and every new flower was a source of delight. The little animals and insects of the field, too, were objects of careful investigation. When it rained Middendorff would tell them stories of the

Greek heroes, or show them the illustrated Bible of Lossius. Campe's *Works for the Young*, too, were a delightful change after the open-air exercises. Sometimes the boys were made to repeat a history in rhyme, of which Ferdinand knew a great deal by heart. Then they would, like the old Greeks, go to war with each other, building Athens or Corinth by the side of the streams, or constructing fortresses with boards and stones from the house that was being pulled down.

The Griesheim boys often came over, and one day they brought their sister Emilie, on which occasion the boys gave a dramatic performance in the loft of the new house. By the end of September the farm-house was ready for the reception of Frau Froebel and her family, consisting of her children, her mother, and aunt. To the boys' great delight an immense waggon of household goods arrived, including cows, pigs, chickens, and other live stock. The new oval table was used for the first time, and cups of cocoa were set round to celebrate the occasion. Frau Froebel and her children moved into the first floor, the ground floor being reserved for the two old ladies.

The combination of households was a great help to Froebel. During the so-called "years of famine" that followed the battle of Leipzig, there was a general scarcity throughout Germany, and Froebel and his sister-in-law had many an anxious hour. Indeed, at first, food was purchased at the price of her silver spoons. The boys made many a meal off the wild fruits growing in the fertile valley, but far from caring about a little pinching, "they ate their dry bread and rancid butter," says Karl Froebel, "with a very good appetite."

A more regular life now began, and Froebel was able to take his part in the lessons. He had had some building bricks made of which the boys were very fond. One afternoon as they lay on the floor playing with them, a thoughtful-looking man of twenty-five suddenly appeared amongst them, and was greeted by all with loud huzzas, for it was Heinrich Langethal, third of our Lutzow trio. He had succeeded in taking orders, to the great satisfaction of his parents, and now determined to spend some months on the study of pedagogy before settling at Keilhau. Langethal was very different from Middendorff and Froebel. He had a stately yet benevolent appearance, and at the same time a voice and manner that gave the impression of firmness. Middendorff was more attractive to women, Langethal to men; it was "a pleasure to see Middendorff; to hear Langethal; and once to have heard him was to trust him for ever." Langethal possessed qualities which were wanting in the other two; Froebel had a productive mind, but little of the higher and more classical culture; this culture was possessed by Middendorff, but it was not of a kind to be useful to young boys. Langethal's classical knowledge was combined with great facility for teaching. He was also a gifted musician.

Froebel was very sensible of the advantage to himself and Middendorff in having such a fellow-worker as Langethal; and Langethal in his turn was so charmed with Froebel's educational venture and with the free, unconventional mode of carrying it out, that he gave up his plans for further preparation, and determined to join his two friends at once. Thus, in the autumn of the year 1817, in the little village of

Keilhau, the three earnest-minded friends, inspired by one thought and aim, started an educational work to which they henceforth devoted all they had of time, strength, and capacity.

Langethal was the means of making the institution more widely known. His position as a scientific man, and his connection both with Berlin and with Erfurt (his birthplace), brought several pupils to the school. His sympathetic manner soon won all hearts, and exercised an excellent influence over the boys. He joined in their games and sang to them Schiller's ballads, and other heroic songs learned on the battle-field. At other times he would stimulate their feeling for chivalry by reading them *The Magic Ring*, which fired their imagination, and inspired them with the determination to become true German knights, like the knights and cavaliers of the middle ages, classical heroes being for the time forgotten.

The utmost energy and zeal was put into the making of cardboard helmets, shields and armour, or wooden arrows, swords and javelins; and they even built limestone forts and castles. Langethal shared their labours, and by the description of the splendour of the German Emperors, inspired them with the hope that one day these glorious times for Germany would come again.

His first effort, however, was to cure the boys of their ugly Thuringian accent, and to teach them correct German.* Corrections by the teacher were found to be insufficient, so a compact was made that

* Mr. Hanschmann gives the following example of their horrible pronunciation: "Die Heiser sind iber der Prigge krehser und heher als die Beime."

every time a boy made a mistake (such as Beime for Baüme, Prigge for Brücke, krehser for grösser) he was to keep silent till he had a chance of correcting someone else, and if he forgot, and spoke, he had to keep silent till he had made two corrections; if he forgot twice, he was banished for ten minutes. Foreign expressions, too, were forbidden, *e.g.*, for the names "Onkel, Tante, Sauce," were substituted "Oheim, Base, Brühe,"* and it was not long before the boys spoke with a fair amount of correctness, and this, together with their little German coats and long hair, gave them a sense of being true German patriots and pioneers in Keilhau.

All foreign drinks, such as tea, coffee, chocolate, were given up, milk or water only being allowed. Simplicity and hardiness ruled in everything. The same clothes served for summer and winter. Excursions were made in all weathers, not excepting snow and storm. The boys walked several miles to the river to skate or bathe. Heat, cold, hunger and thirst, were borne without a murmur. For the sake of a game at hunting they would climb the Kolmwald whilst the storm roared in the valley below. Langethal was the leader in these wild games; Middendorff and Froebel would occasionally go with them, Froebel's way being to instruct the boys on the road, whilst Middendorff would fill them with admiration for the beauty of the country. Heinr. Langethal would carry the boys off on some wild excursion during the day, and bring them back to Middendorff's poetical influence in the evening, whilst Froebel was the one to suggest improvements and reforms. In the evenings they would sing,

* The dear old ladies, however, refused to be called "Gross-basen."

Middendorff joining in with his sweet tenor voice, and Froebel with his harsher bass. Sometimes they would busy themselves with cardboard work, whilst one of the teachers read aloud. Froebel was full of fun at such times. It will be seen that the life at Keilhau at this time was more like that of a noble brotherhood than of a school. The very individuality of these three excellent men had its distinct educational influence on the boys. Froebel's endeavour was to apply the principles of human development to all the instruction given to his boys, to find indeed the Philosopher's Stone in education. He was beset with practical difficulties, and these were not easily solved. But as far as his teaching and methods went, he succeeded from the very first. No deadening and stultifying methods were possible with him. He always found a way of awakening the intelligence and stimulating the self-activity of his boys, so that their knowledge, as far as it went, was their own. We have two excellent accounts of this time, one by Langethal's young brother Christian, who, whilst extolling Froebel's principles, does not omit to point out certain errors in his practice.*

At first the whole direction of the children's education devolved upon Froebel.‡ "Froebel's methods," says Christian Langethal, "were very original, and no doubt his errors are due to this originality." His endeavour was to fix upon some central principle round which all instruction and education should

* "Where there is much light, there will also be much shadow." "Err we must, but each effort of our aspirations brings us nearer to the truth."—GOETHE.

‡ Langethal was as yet too little acquainted with the Froebel methods, and Middendorff was a very echo of Froebel.

revolve; which should, in short, harmonise and bring into one organic whole the teacher's efforts. Froebel's keystone is the self-activity of the learner. The natural means for the stimulation of self-activity are simple objects. The thorough knowledge of such objects is the best and the most natural starting-point for further advancement. In everything the familiar should come first, and lead to the unfamiliar. The knowledge of a thing should be emphasised and completed by the careful study of its parts, even to the utmost detail, and these parts should be arranged in logical sequence.* Again Froebel maintained that you only know a thing when you can teach it; so he made his pupils teach again what they had learned, hunting up all they could find on the subject. This could hardly be called instruction, but it implied the principle that the pupil should express his own conception of what he learns. To Pestalozzi's grand contribution towards education, *i.e.*, Anschauung, Froebel added expression. Expression in its utmost variety, expression by words and by a great variety of action, such as singing, moving, drawing, etc.; expression in accordance with the character of the individual; self-expression by self-activity. But Froebel had no more reached the whole truth than Pestalozzi. He was still struggling, and "to struggle means to err."

Christian Langethal recalls a characteristic scene of this time. Langethal and Middendorf were leaning

---

* Christian Langethal, whilst lauding Froebel's logic and thoroughness, says that in the subjects best known to him he dwelt too much on details, and that in his endeavour after order he often erred on the side of pedantry.

against the stove* listening with all their eyes and ears, whilst Froebel, marching up and down the room, was giving them instruction in educational methods. The children caught a word here and there, such as self-activity, observation, intuition, going from the known to the unknown; and one of them whispered, "I suppose they are learning to march." The endeavour to keep to a logical sequence in the subjects of instruction, and to proceed only from the known to the unknown, made the acquisition of actual knowledge very slow, and often led to a "terrible thoroughness" which gave the impression that nothing was learned at Keilhau. "It took quite two years" says Christian Langethal, "to lay the foundation-stone of knowledge." Keilhau was certainly not the place in which to cultivate hot-house plants. But in spite of this apparent want of result, the public placed such confidence in the institution as to bring to it, not unfrequently, pupils who were doing no good elsewhere. For all such Keilhau found a remedy, though it could not be expected to provide faculties that nature had denied. Froebel's nephew, Karl, has left some "recollections" of his uncle, published in 1872. He praises in the highest degree Froebel's extreme order and method. He says that the two subjects he learned with his uncle† made a lasting impression on him, and awakened to an unusual degree the interest and activity of the class. He gives the following example of a language lesson:

"Look round and tell me what you see."
"Table, chair, window, door, book, boy."

---

* The stove was nearly always cold or smoking.
† Form and Language, taught on the Pestalozzian method.

"Write all that down."

That is how Froebel began, standing before the pupils with eager face and long black hair, whilst they waited with curiosity to see what could be learned from such common things.

"What do all these words mean?" Long silence, then mumbling, the pupils at sea.

"All these words indicate objects or things; repeat what I say; write it."

"Objects" sounded rather mysterious to them.

"An object is a thing outside of yourself."

"Now tell me some objects you have seen but which you cannot see at this moment. Write them down. What are all these words?"

A second time they could not say, so they had to repeat, "These words are names of objects which can be perceived."

Froebel continued, "A perceptible object, which, however, we do not perceive but only remember, is only in our minds, it is a representation. We may have an image in our minds of things not seen by us or others, not possible to be seen." Karl Froebel does not tell us whether such examples as phœnix, griffin, dragon, sphinx, good or bad spirits, were mentioned. But they went on to discuss how certain things come to be perceived, such as the air, the odour of flowers, storm, cold, heat, living things, dead things, stuffed things, the pulse, musical instruments, etc., and many were led to reflect on their own conception of life itself, which you can neither see, hear, taste, feel, nor smell."

"After having made their lists during the first few lessons, they were asked to classify the objects according to their similarities or differences, and they soon learned to place them under such headings as animals, plants, stones, human beings, utensils, tools, buildings, materials, etc., and to write under them, 'all these objects are plants—animals'—and the rest. This classification of objects suggested to them the variety in the physical world, and the boys soon arrived at the conclusion that all objects are either natural, artificial, or a combination of these."

"From the objects the children learned to describe verbally, and in writing, their qualities, and so to discriminate and name colour, light, taste, smell, warmth, movement, material condition, and alteration. Further exercises consisted in making lists of qualities belonging to the same object, or of those common to several objects; of predicatory verbs applicable to a given subject—as the sun shines, warms, illumines. Or they might be asked to compare the power of resistance in different objects, such as sand, wood, stone,* or the actions characteristic of living creatures, or words relating to time or space. These logical exercises were never long enough to weary the children. Indeed, they took great pleasure in them, and would often discuss them out of school."

After these preliminary exercises the pupils were handed over to Langethal for more formal grammar studies, and to begin Greek and later on Latin. Langethal followed Herbart's† order of teaching languages, *i.e.*, Greek before Latin.

---

* Verifying by experiment wherever it was possible. Everything was made real; indeed, there was at this time no school so thoroughly Pestalozzian as Froebel's at Keilhau.

† Johann Friedrich Herbart (1776 to 1841) had left Göttingen in 1809, two years before Froebel's arrival there, and was now at Koenigsberg. According to Professor Reiss, Herbart's service to education was

At Christmas time some friends in the north sent "a Christmas present for the little ones at Keilhau." They had as yet only one large room completed. This served as play-room, sitting-room, and class-room, and the same table was used for work, play, lessons, and food. In this room they held their Christmas festival, the great and glad event being the setting of a stove, which the teachers themselves had built to replace the old one, which had always smoked.

Two important events for Froebel happened in the summer of 1818. In June he came into possession of the farm,* whilst his sister-in-law moved to Volkstaedt; and on the 20th September he married a lady of about the same age as himself, whom he had met in Berlin, Fräulein Wilhelmine Hofmeister, an earnest student of Schleiermacher and Fichte. She entered heartily into Froebel's plans, and proved to be a most devoted and suitable wife.

Her friends were at first unwilling for her to leave her somewhat luxurious home, and enter upon a life of struggle and privation; but to Froebel's great joy she overcame their objections, and the marriage took place on her birthday. Frau Froebel had an adopted

two-fold :—From ethics he deduced the universal end of education. From scientific psychology (which he opposed to the "faculty psychology") the practical directions for reaching the end. Herbart maintains that the formation of a good will is the end of education; the means by which the end is to be attained are government, discipline, and instruction. The special function of government is to command and restrain, and so form good and prevent bad habits, before self-government is possible. The special function of discipline is to work upon the feelings in such a way that the child may be influenced to voluntary good actions. The special function of instruction is so to multiply and organise ideas that many-sided duly-balanced interest may arise—interest which makes most for character.

* At Keilhau.

daughter, Ernestine Crispine, who accompanied her to Keilhau, and ultimately became the wife of Langethal.

The arrival of these ladies was a great source of happiness to Froebel; but the boys soon saw that they were no longer the chief centre of interest. The teachers, instead of sitting at the oval table with them as formerly, now took their places at a separate table with Herr and Frau Froebel; and still worse, a table and five chairs for afternoon coffee* were placed on the playground, which had been levelled and prepared by the boys themselves.

In spite of all this, however, they soon discovered the good qualities of the "Berlin lady." She was a woman of taste and character, a beautiful reader, and an enthusiastic student of German literature and natural science.

Her accomplishments and personal character added much to the culture and happiness of the Froebel home. With all her learning she was modest and unpretending, and entered with the utmost cheerfulness and unselfishness into the frugal simplicity of school life, abstaining from many little comforts to which she had been accustomed.†

The evenings of this winter were spent by the boys on cardboard work, whilst the teachers would read to them the Nibelungen Lied in the old German dialect; and as Christmas approached the womanly influence was found to be a great resource. The decorations were

---

* This luxury, however, was only indulged in occasionally, as it was in direct opposition to the training to hardihood and simplicity to which Froebel had accustomed the boys.

† It was a pity that Frau Froebel's domestic capabilities were not equal to her general culture and goodwill. As the school grew larger it was more and more in need of a good practical manager.

much more beautiful than they had been on the previous Christmas; the distempered walls were hung with branches and illuminated by Christmas candles, and the presents (provided by a good friend at the castle) were hidden amongst the foliage. This green Christmas room served for some days as a shelter for some poor little robins and sparrows who came in search of food, and received their share of the Christmas dainties. There were twelve boys by this time, and now for the first time they had a room of their own.

Many joys were in store for the children this winter, one especially, the new snow-slide behind the "long garden"; the little sledges went down this run with lightning speed. There was also a new exercise ground, but this had less attraction for them. Langethal gave some exercises for the limbs, hands, and even for every finger, which Froebel had arranged progressively, and which the boys were inclined to think were too thorough. These exercises were published by Spiess. Those Froebel considered suitable for infants are included in the *Mutter-und Kose-Lieder*.

In the spring of 1819 (the tercentenary of the Reformation) Froebel and Langethal joined a memorial for the erection of a statue to Martin Luther. Froebel further suggested that the best memorial to Luther's memory would be to provide an education for his descendants, if any could be found. Liberal contributions were sent from Berlin and Jena. In consequence of this two boys—Johann Georg, aged eighteen, and Joh. Ernst, aged thirteen—were placed in the Froebel School: they were the descendants of Luther's brother.*

* Their father, Joh. Nik. Luther, a shepherd, bore a great resemblance to the Reformer.

The elder boy was of a serious and aspiring nature, and became a pastor; the younger a stone-cutter. In the following year (1820) Froebel's lease at Hainhold's came to an end, and he was at a loss to know what to do until he could find the means to complete the school building. At this crisis his brother Christian, who had confidence in his work, decided to give up his business at Osterode, and move to Keilhau with his family and belongings. This timely help on his brother's part probably saved Froebel's school. Five members were added to the little colony—Brother Christian, his wife, and three daughters, aged respectively nineteen, eighteen, and six.*

The only sitting-room available for the Christian Froebels was a large wash-house, and this had also to serve as a place in which to assemble the whole school.

It was in this large room that they all spent their Christmas of the year 1820, for they did not move properly into the school-house till June, 1821, when, through Christian Froebel's substantial and timely help, the building was completed.

At this time the number of adults in the institution, exclusive of the servants, was twenty-five, that of the pupils sixteen; four more were added by the end of the year, their ages ranging from seven to eighteen. In 1822 six new pupils came, and dwelling-rooms for Froebel and his teachers were completed, whilst the house, hitherto occupied in a half-furnished state, was put into thorough repair, and fitted up as a home for

* Albertina afterwards married Middendorff, Emilie became Barop's second wife, and Elisa, the youngest, married Barop's friend, Doctor Schaffner.

the elder brother and his family; and the school began to flourish.

In 1823 Johann Arnold Barop (son of a lawyer in Dortmund) and his wife joined the Keilhau community. He had studied theology at Halle, but, like Langethal, he was so attracted by the Froebel spirit that he also determined to join in the work. With the exception of a year's military service in Berlin, and the time he worked for Froebel in Switzerland, Barop hardly ever left Keilhau again; and it was he who succeeded to the school after Froebel's death. Sixteen new pupils entered in 1824, and further building was required. This building included a large dining-hall, in which Froebel conducted his Christmas service at the end of the year.

The most prosperous years for the school were from 1824-26, when the pupils numbered fifty-six. In addition to the teachers there were eight assistants in the school, including George Luther and Ferdinand Froebel, who were by this time pupil teachers.[*] Several teachers of distinction were added to the staff. Schoenbein, best known as a physicist, undertook the direction of the science teaching in the school;[†] Herzog, a well-known philologist, the language teach-teaching; and Michaelis, the geography. He was summoned to Würtemberg in 1824 to make a topographical map of the Black Forest, on which occasion Julius Froebel acted as his assistant. Karl Froebel left Keilhau about the same time. Froebel regretted

---

[*] Froebel often did too much in this way, and his liberality did not always meet with the gratitude it deserved.

[†] Schoenbein was also the inventor of gun-cotton and the discoverer of ozone.

losing these nephews, the more that they had been somewhat set against him by Herzog.* The separation thus caused between uncle and nephews continued till quite recently, when Karl has shown renewed interest in his uncle's work by publishing his *Recollections of Keilhau*. Karl Froebel was for some time the Principal of a High School for Girls, established at Hamburg in 1848, and subsequently he settled at Edinburgh, where he worked zealously for eduation. Julius, the eldest son of Christoph Froebel, distinguished himself both in science and literature. He was the author of a *Complete Guide to Physical Geography*, and was, for a time, Professor at the Mineralogical College at Zurich. He published, in 1843, a book on Chrystallography, which won him some renown. He studied at Jena and Berlin, and was a great traveller.

The condition of Froebel's school in 1825 may be gathered from the following report by Inspector Zeh:— "The two days I have spent in the institution and lived its life have been to me interesting, instructive, and enjoyable. They have served only to confirm and increase my respect for the school and its principal, by whose unselfishness, zeal, and fidelity it has been carried on. The free yet disciplined tone that exists amongst the boys in and out of school hours is most refreshing. The institution presents a harmony of life that is rarely met with;—a family of sixty members, living in intimate, peaceful association, all doing heartily what they have to do, putting complete confidence in each other, every member contributing his share to the whole, so that the work goes on of itself. The master

---

* Herzog seems to have behaved very badly to Froebel, and to have caused him much trouble.

of the school is loved by all. The little ones clamour round his knee, whilst he consults with his teachers, as friends and equals, and shows a wisdom and a zeal for the good cause, which never fails to command their respect and reverence. This close bond of union amongst their elders exercises the best possible influence on the boys, which is shown by their unquestioning submission and affection, and by the excellence of their discipline. I saw nothing during my stay at Keilhau of the nature of reproach or punishment. No sooner was school over than the children rushed joyously into the fresh air. Yet there was no roughness or rudeness. The boys were called by their Christian names, and all seemed to be equals, free in their brotherhood, obedient to a law within. They conducted their own games, but there was always a teacher amongst them, sometimes joining the game, and submitting like the rest to its rules. This complex family life promotes an all-round stimulation of the faculties and an education of individuality which are most striking. The strong assist the weak, so that there is neither tyranny nor injustice. The boys quickly check any insubordination on the part of a playmate by leaving him out of the game till he submits; and thus they control and educate each other, and are free and active in mind and body. The youngest pupils are only five years of age. These learn to observe the things presented to them, and to name them properly, and to collect, in a pleasant way, such intellectual mites for future use as suits their present powers. The main principle observed throughout the school is the stimulation of individual activity. How different is this from the treatment of the young mind as if it were a money-box in which to hoard all kinds of coin. Here instruction proceeds slowly, step by step, according to the laws of mental association. There is no trifling; none of the foolish philanthropy which provides an alphabet made in sweets to be eaten. The children pass from the simple to the complex, from the concrete to the abstract, in such natural order that they go to their learning as happily as to their play. Indeed, I was a witness of the fact that the little ones, whose lessons had been somewhat disturbed by my arrival, went to ask Froebel whether they were not going to have 'lessons like the big ones.' The most advanced part of the classical instruction is about equal to what the first class would take in a grammar school. Last winter the boys read Plato, Horace, and Demosthenes, and translated Cornelius Nepos into Greek. On my first visit I gave my chief attention to the younger children, and could not help wishing that all our elementary schools were taught in this way. And no less was my admiration awakened by the classical instruction given to the elder boys, which only began in 1820, but which already shows an admirable thoroughness. I saw everything possible in the time allowed me, and was delighted both by the instruction and the education given in this establishment. Froebel's object is not knowledge or science, but a free, self-active development of the mind, which takes intelligent account of everything presented to it. All that is done conduces to the development of power in the child. The object of these teachers is to stimulate the thought of the pupil, and give, as it were, a kind of mental gymnastics. The dead grammar is made to live; for with the language the children receive instruction in the character and customs of the people speaking it. It is well for those children who are educated here from their sixth year. I would that all schools could be turned into such educational homes as this! Were this the case, we should in a few generations become a stronger and nobler race."*

On the 16th September of this year (1825) there was great rejoicing in the little colony, for a double betrothal took place, *i.e.*, that of Langethal with Frau Froebel's foster-daughter, Ernestine, and of Middendorff with Christian Froebel's eldest daughter, Albertina.†

The religious teaching in the school was excellent. Froebel was not much wedded to forms and ceremonies, but he came of a pious stock, and was inspired by a truly Christian spirit. He and his pupils joined the congregation at Keilhau, and contributed not a little to the religious life of the place. His boys joined the village boys in the preparation for confirmation, and were addressed by the minister with the familiar pronoun " du." They generally walked to Eichfeld to church, but on wet days they attended the little church at Keilhau. Brave young Luther‡ attended in the morning at Eichfeld, and in the afternoon at Keilhau; Middendorff nodding his approval at the thoroughness of the young fellow.

The learning by heart was limited to a few texts of Scripture, but the boys never missed the prayer and

---

* This report, by an inspector sent for the purpose by the Prussian Government, regarded as an unprejudiced expression of judgment, ought to have gone far to militate against the unjust condemnation of the Keilhau Institution which followed.

† The happy couples were married in the spring of the next year.

‡ He went to the Tuebingen University in 1825.

hymn morning and evening, and their walks were often utilised by Froebel to awaken a spirit of reverence. For an understanding of the careful religious instruction given in the school, we would refer the reader to a pamphlet by Froebel, published at Erfurt in 1821, entitled *An education thoroughly adapted to the needs of the German character*. It seems extraordinary to those who have studied Froebel's life, to find he should ever have been accused of irreligion. But, alas! this sorrow came to him.

The main part of Froebel's literary effort lies between the year 1820, when his brother Christian joined him, and 1826, when he summed up and amplified his previous writings in the *Education of Man*.

We have, however, in addition to this, a series of articles in a little weekly paper, called *Das Sonntagsblatt*, published between 1837 and 1840, and his *Mother's Play Songs*, published in 1843. Also, in 1850, several articles in a paper called *Die Wochenschrift*, edited by Dr. Wichard Lange.

CHAPTER VI.

TROUBLED TIMES.

1826 TO 1829. KEILHAU, GÖTTINGEN.

The Coming Storm—Devoted Band of Educationists—Political Trouble—Money Troubles—Froebel's Friendship with Krause—Educational Friends in Göttingen—Comparison of Krause's and Froebel's Principles of Education—Krause and Contemporary Philosophers—Scheme for an Industrial School—Castle of Helba—Froebel's Kindergarten Occupations—Failure of the Scheme.

INSPECTOR ZEH'S report to the Council of Schwarzburg-Rudolstadt did no more than justice to the excellence of the Keilhau institution. But the demand for a report of the school was in itself a sign of the coming storm. The school had by this time become popular; its numbers had increased rapidly, and it had need of a practical ability and organising power, unfortunately not possessed by any of the band of heroes who devoted their time, their strength, and their money to the realisation of a noble idea. Had Froebel or his wife possessed any business capacity they might have foreseen the troubles that would arise out of the growing needs of the little community, and the constant additions to the school building. As it was, although Middendorff had sacrificed his little inheritance, it was only a drop in the ocean of that which was necessary to complete the buildings and pay the ground-rent; and even Christian Froebel's income, which he gave up entirely for the institution, was insufficient to stave off increasing debts. Barop would willingly have poured his small income into the common purse, but his father refused to hand it up.

And these troubles were increased by the political agitations of the time. The democratic spirit, which had caused so much disturbance in 1815, was still rife, and the Government naturally looked with suspicion on all movements that advocated freedom of thought. Froebel's views on education, though they were characterised by the utmost partriotism, were unfortunately confounded with the ideas of liberty and equality that underlay so many political agitations at this time. Hence it was thought that Keilhau was a refuge for demagogues; Barop innocently contributed to this confusion. His political views had got him into trouble at Halle, and his papers were seized, and though nothing compromising was found in them, the Prussian Government continued to maintain a suspicious attitude towards him and his colleagues. This gave a handle to those who differed from them in their social or religious views, and some of their enemies clamoured for a suspension of the school. The Duke of Rudolstadt, however, bearing in mind Inspector Zeh's excellent report, refused to add his authority for this, and merely requested Froebel for the present to do away with the old German costume, which was similar to that worn by the social-democrats. This he consented to do, much to the astonishment of the boys, and the displeasure of many of the parents, who made the foolish reports about the school an excuse for withdrawing their children and their patronage. Herzog, a teacher, unfortunately added to Froebel's troubles by inducing his three nephews to leave the school just at a time when they might have comforted and supported their uncle in his difficulties. But Froebel continued undismayed in the prosecution of his ideas, and, in pure simplicity and singleness of heart, expected no less than utter self-annihilation on the part of his colleagues. But their utmost devotion could not stave off money troubles. At length came the moment when the funds were inadequate to carry on the daily work; the numbers in the school diminished so rapidly that of sixty pupils there remained in 1829 only five. Creditors were impatient, and it wanted all Middendorff's conciliatory powers to keep them from personal attacks on Froebel. Sometimes, indeed, his teachers would send him out of the house the back way, whilst they used all possible persuasion to keep the creditors quiet. All shared in this difficult task. Wichard Lange tells a touching anecdote of a locksmith, who, on being urged by his lawyer to "prosecute the fellows," replied with horror, "that he would rather lose his hardly earned money than doubt the honour of such men, and that nothing would persuade him to add to their trouble."

In spite of these troubles Froebel kept up his courage, and never lost sight of his object. "Do not be dismayed at the attitude of Berlin or the world towards our movement," he wrote to Barop in 1827; "only keep firm and steadfast. That which I had but seen in a dream or vision, as it were, is now clear and evident. The divine order in creation and throughout the natural world is our pattern for the education of man. It is for us to defend the rights of nature in education."

Neither Middendorff nor the other teachers wavered in their fidelity to Froebel and to the cause; they only clung the more to their mission and their hopes. At a time when their funds were at the lowest, they celebrated the betrothal of Barop and Emilie Froebel.* It was feared that their union might take them away from Keilhau, but, in spite of the unpromising outlook, they assured their friends that it was their intention to stay. The marriage took place in 1831.

Froebel's educational idea had attracted the attention of the philosopher Krause,† and he sent Froebel a copy of his works. There was, he thought, a remarkable agreement in principle between himself and Froebel. The vigorous correspondence that followed no doubt exercised a strong influence on Froebel, and helped to clear his ideas. Krause's views of the universe (arrived at rather from a scholarly than from a practical point of view) only served to confirm Froebel in the soundness of his educational idea. In his correspondence Krause had objected to Froebel's application of the term national or German to his educational scheme, declaring it to be thoroughly human rather than German; and this question formed the subject of their first interview. To Froebel it

---

* Christian Froebel's second daughter. It was Barop who, in 1829, valiantly came to the rescue of a sinking ship, and by sheer energy and devotion steered her through the storm and struggle, and got her into still waters again.

† Karl Christian Friederich Krause, 1781 to 1832.

seemed that the apparent pretentiousness of the term "purely human" would give even more offence than the expression he had used. Froebel's great wish (and this might almost be called Krausean) was to form, with his friends, a social community, living a common life. A life "in harmony with the will of God, the beauty of nature, and the needs of man; a life that would reconcile body and mind, sense and reason, will and deed, and be in short the exemplification of one divine law."

His desire to make the personal acquaintance of the philosopher took him and Middendorff to Göttingen in the summer holidays of 1828. By Krause they were introduced to Dr. Hermann von Leonhardi, afterwards Professor at the University of Prague, but at this time a student at Göttingen. Also to the Frankenbergs of Eddigehausen, the younger members of the family being ardent disciples of Krause. Thus Froebel had the most favourable opportunity of making Krause's acquaintance and hearing his views. It was Krause who induced Froebel to study Comenius.* Krause and Herder had endeavoured in 1811 to draw attention to Comenius in *The Journal of Human Life*. Krause maintained that the *Panegersia* proposed an entirely new basis of education, made it, in short, an art. "It is an attempt," he said, "to find a method of education, consciously based upon science, whereby teachers will teach less and learners learn more; whereby there will be less noise in the schools, less distaste, fewer idle pupils, more happiness and progress; whereby

* Johann Amos Comenius, 1592 to 1671.

confusion, division, and darkness will give place to order, intelligence, and peace. Comenius," he said, "was the first advocate of Pestalozzi's doctrine of Anschauung." Krause looked upon Froebel as the educational successor of Pestalozzi and Comenius. Froebel, he thought, might show, as it had never been shown before, how the Pestalozzian doctrine of Anschauung was to be applied to the education of every child.

Leonhardi describes the appearance of our two friends on their arrival at Göttingen. "There was," he says, "a total absence of any attempt at elegance, and their simple straightforward manner sometimes repelled strangers. Froebel had an almost Eastern type of countenance, with his large, protruding ears, long nose, low forehead, and small eyes. He was very serious; had a curious and fantastic way of looking at things and of expressing himself, so that he was not always understood. Middendorff and Langethal, on the other hand, in spite of their old German costume and long hair parted in the middle, always made a pleasing impression. To the superficial, Froebel's simplicity of nature appeared childish; others, better able to read beneath the surface, were impressed with his love of human nature and indefatigable zeal and energy." Amongst his admirers we may count the naturalist, Karl Schimpfer, Professor Ahrens of Heidelberg, and Krause himself.

Froebel found in Krause's philosophy much that was entirely in harmony with his own views on education. Indeed, it seemed to him but a more scientific expression of his main principle; for Krause required a complete and harmonious development of the human being, based on a scientific study of his nature and place in the universe—in short, the art of life based upon science. The unity of life, too, which Froebel had always insisted on, was here clearly expressed. "Education," says Krause, "consists in such a scientific training of man's powers and inner life as will enable him to express his spirituality." The art of education, according to Krause, consists in bringing the subjective and objective conditions of life into one organic, harmonious whole. The human being has need of education from the moment he enters life, and continues to need it as long as any of his faculties remain undeveloped. Individuals, families, races, and even the whole humanity, so long as they are but partially developed, have need of it. Krause gives, as an instance of the grotesque in education, the common practice of training an otherwise uneducated man for some speciality. "The need of objective education ends when the learner has learned to educate himself. As every being has that within him which is common to all humanity, as well as that which is peculiar to him as an individual, it is evident that his development concerns itself both with that which he has in common with all men, and with that which is peculiar to him as an individual. Not only must we abstain from hindering free development, but this freedom of development must be fostered and strengthened to the utmost, for on it will depend the chief factor in the child's education, *i.e.*, his self-activity and instinct for productiveness." Krause regards the stimulation of self-activity and individuality as the very essence of a true education, the object of which is to produce a "perfectly harmonised life."

'A human being may have certain of his faculties more or less fully developed, but whilst any remain immature, he is, as regards these, a child in need of education; and the same may be said of families, nations, and of humanity generally. The child must be trained through his self-activity to control himself and his surroundings, and thus to make the world his own, himself being a harmonious part of it. The harmoniously-developed man is the most lovable creature in the world, and at the same time the most striking image of the divine. The educator must be free from egotism; he must respect both his pupil and himself: maybe he has before him one greater than himself. Let him not seek for more than spontaneous submission to his authority. For him it is to exercise unlimited love and patience. Let the sacredness of his office help him to overcome its difficulties. Let the means and methods he employs be in accord with all that is good and true and beautiful, so that his pupil see in him an ideal of affection and nobility."*

Dr. Hermann von Leonhardi, the editor of Krause's works, says: "Some suppose that Krause was a mere follower of Schelling, but this is an error. It is true that he endeavoured to reconcile the philosophy of Schelling, which makes thought an attribute of nature, with that of Fichte, which makes nature an attribute of thought. His own view was that both nature and intellect originate in God. But Krause's system was original. It combines the best points of Plato and Aristotle; of idealism and realism. Krause has indeed contributed much to the science, ethics, art, and religion of our time."

* KRAUSE's *Urbild der Menschheit.*

Krause and Froebel were at one in their demand for an education such as would strengthen and bring out the spiritual nature of man. They also agreed in placing the Pestalozzian principle of self-activity at the very basis of their educational systems. Froebel's social scheme was simpler and more practical than Krause's, being based solely upon Pestalozzi's three-fold relationship of man, *i.e.*, his relationship to God, to nature, and to his fellow-man.* Froebel has done great service to education in his clear demonstration of these three relationships from the very beginning of human life, and in the graduated series of objects he has devised for the training of the child in these three directions. He has, however, no special object teaching; with him all training is of a kind to develop sense, reason, imagination, and originality. His main point was not arrived at from the study of speculative philosophy, but from his observation of nature. It was based upon his experience of the real rather than upon his conception of the ideal. His object was the continuous, unremitting development of man as an organic whole.

There are no leaps in nature, and neither must there be in education. The educator must adapt his methods to the natural development of the child, and be ready to revise them whenever desirable.

Krause's system was slow in making its way in Germany. Had he had a professorship at one of the universities he would probably, like Hegel,† have established an influential school. As it was, he was

---

* Comenius had taken as his three-fold basis of education the world, God, and reason.

† His rival for the Fichte professorship in Berlin.

ignored, because, according to Heinrich Ahrens, "his system was not in harmony with the theories of Kant and Hegel, nor with the rationalism and materialism into which these philosophies merged. The contrasting views urged by the followers of one or other of these philosophers found many hearers, being more readily understood than the doctrines which treat philosophy on a broader basis. Krause's system is an adaptation of philosophy to human life. It is in harmony with Christian principles and social progress, its object being to develop all that is good and noble in human nature."

Froebel sent Krause the first copy of his scheme for a national school. Such a school he felt would express his views more fully than was possible, even in his own school at Keilhau. He had written to Herr Inspector Zeh, in 1827, hoping that through his influence a locale for such an experiment might be obtained; and though he failed in this, his friends succeeded in interesting the Duke of Meiningen (one of the most enterprising princes of his time) in his work. It happened that the Duke's physician, Dr. Hohebaum, a most enlightened educationist, had been at Keilhau, and he now proposed that the Duke should establish a people's school at Helba, and that Froebel should be asked to present a scheme for it. To this end an interview was brought about between the Prince and Froebel, in consequence of which he worked out, with his friends at Keilhau, a model scheme of education.

Various kinds of hand-work, *e.g.* weaving, carpentering, gardening, were to form a substantial part of the scheme. This practical work was intended to stimulate the children's interest and intelligence, and at the same time to train them to habits of industry and dexterity. They were to learn by doing, and to become productive members of society. The materials used were frequently to form the subject of lessons, which were to be so graded as to form an educational whole, and lay the foundation for a happy, industrious, and thrifty life.

In addition to the boys' school there was to be :—

1. A nursery-room for orphans under seven years of age.
2. An elementary school.
3. A technical school for the development of German art and industry.
4. A school for mothers.

The institution at Keilhau was to form part of the scheme by preparing pupils for more special studies.

Pestalozzi's *Intuitive Method* was to be adopted in its entirety.

The scheme was presented to the Duke, and he decided to hand over to Froebel his estate of Helba, with thirty acres of ground, and a subsidy of about £80 a year.* Needless to say this quasi-public recognition of his work was a source of great rejoicing to Froebel and his friends at Keilhau. They had for many years been content to work hand in hand in comparative obscurity. Here was a chance of proving the value of the Froebel idea. The Castle of Helba stands in beautiful grounds, in a sunny valley of the Thuringian Forest, not far from Meiningen. The region is rich in animals and plants suitable for nature lessons, and has many points of historical interest.

* 1000 gulden.

In a letter to Barop, dated March, 1828, Froebel says: "For some time my thoughts have been occupied with the problem of the right education for children between three and seven years of age. Various influences have now determined me to make the training of motherless children of this age part of the work done at Helba. We shall begin with those of the middle classes. I shall not call this an infant school, because I do not intend the children to be schooled, but to be allowed under the gentlest treatment to develop freely."

This scheme is valuable because it expresses fully Froebel's educational idea. His object is to connect observation and expression, thought and deed, sense-impression, knowledge and faculty. He bases all learning upon self-activity and self-expression, and holds that there is much valuable training for children in home and school duties, in the collection of objects for illustrating natural history lessons, in gardening, in decorating, and in cleaning. Training and instruction were to go hand in hand. Many of the occupations devised for the people's school at Helba have, through the Kindergarten, become familiar to us. They are such as produce skill of eye and hand, and develop in the children a sense of symmetry, harmony, and beauty. Nearly a hundred Kindergarten games were added to the occupations.

Froebel was consulted by the Duke of Meiningen with regard to the education of his only son and heir, and he strongly urged that the young prince should be educated *with other boys.* This gave umbrage to the former directors of the boy's education; and, prompted by jealousy, they did what they could to throw discredit on the new scheme, and on the Keilhau institution itself. The good Duke was disturbed by this conflict, and began to waver and to retreat, in so far as to limit the number of pupils to be educated with his son; and as under these conditions it was not possible for Froebel to carry out his idea in its entirety, he decided with the utmost regret to give up the plan, and to content himself for the present with the mere conception of it. It was not fruitless, however, for the germs of much of his future work are to be found in the Helba scheme.

PART II.
THE KINDERGARTEN

CHAPTER VII.
SWITZERLAND.

1830 TO 1836. FRANKFURT, WARTENSEE, WILLISAU, BURGDORF.

Barop—The Holzhausens—Wartensee—The New Institution—Froebel in Switzerland—Enemies—Chequer Drawing—Johann Gottlieb Fichte—Womanly Influence—Schnyder—Barop in Switzerland—The Frankenberg Family—Willisau Religious Persecution—Sudden Attack—Public Examination—Seasonable Help—Froebel's Authority—Burgdorf—Picturesque Situation—Success of the New Education—Its Influence on Home Life—Training of the Mother—Langethal's View—Frau Froebel's Illness—New Arrangements—Leonhardi and Krause—Spread of Froebelism.

FROEBEL'S *Education of Man*, published in 1826, at a time when he was suffering so much from difficulties within and without, gives the fullest expression we possess of his idea of education. It was entirely based upon Pestalozzi's principle of "Anschauung," with the addition of his own special doctrine of "Darstellung," or *living out* that which has been *taken in*. As Mr. Hanschmann remarks, "America was not named after Columbus," and it is possible that Froebel has not yet received the credit due to him as the originator of this doctrine. Surely it is of equal importance with that of Auschauung itself. For until we have expressed that which we have observed and understood, it is hardly our own. By "Darstellung" Froebel does not mean mere verbal expression, but rather what might be called exhaustive expression, *i.e.*, expression in every variety of way, and by every kind of activity. This is best seen in a good Kindergarten, where the child's doings throughout are made to focus on the subject before him so as to give him as real and complete an idea as possible.

In the spring of 1831, Froebel sent his friends in Frankfurt his *Outlines of Education*, and the Helba scheme which contained the germs of the future Kindergarten. Hereupon followed a correspondence, which he hoped would not only clear his system of all that was vague or unpractical, but would gain friends for the cause.

"All may join in this noble work," he wrote, "rich and poor, old and young, great and small. For its object is to educate the human being in harmony with his nature and the conditions of his time." The little community at Keilhau led an ideal life of devotion to the cause and to each other; and the difficulties they had to encounter in consequence of their money troubles, and Herzog's disloyalty, only served to strengthen the bond between them.

In May, 1831, Froebel went to Frankfurt-am-Main, to see his many friends. There was Gruner, who had started him in his educational career; Frau von Holzhausen, who had from the first so thoroughly understood and sympathised with his aspirations. With men of thought and intelligence Froebel's genius always made itself felt, and indeed few remained altogether indifferent to him. Some, it is true, were repelled by his peculiar manner and self-assertion; but by far the larger number were attracted by his utter belief in his idea.

At the Holzhausens' he met the accomplished

musician and composer Xavier Schnyder, of Wartensee (1786 to 1868), who, as a man of culture, as well as an experienced teacher and educationist, was in a position to appreciate Froebel's scheme of education. He himself had worked with Pestalozzi, was a friend of the musician Naegeli, and of Jean Paul Richter.

Schnyder went carefully through the scheme drawn up by Froebel and his Keilhau friends, and was so much impressed with the value and importance of the work and the originality of its founder, that, to Froebel's great delight, he offered to put at his disposal the Castle of Wartensee (Lake of Sempach), in Switzerland. Thither Froebel and Middendorff proceeded in July, and by the 12th August they had received from the Minister of Education authorisation to start a Froebel school in the Canton of Lucerne. This authorisation took the form of the following letter, addressed

"To Herrn Schnyder, of Wartensee.

"Honoured Sir,—We have the pleasure of sending you and Herrn Friedrich Froebel the decision of the Council which met on the 10th inst., and which authorises you to establish in the Canton a private model school such as you have described. We congratulate the Canton on the prospect of having a school under such excellent management, and one which is likely to have so good an influence on the other schools of the Canton. We shall have the honour to interest ourselves especially in this institution, and at all times be ready to do anything in our power to further so beneficent an undertaking.

"We are, dear sir, respectfully yours,
"E. Pfyffer and N. Ruettimann,
"In the name of the President and Council of Education,
"Lucerne, August 12th, 1831."

A circular dated August 3rd, 1831, announced the opening of "The Wartensee Institution," which was intended for the German, French, and Italian children of the surrounding cantons. German, however, was to be the language in use. The pupils were to be prepared for trade, commerce, or the university. The castle, with its furniture, its silver, its magnificent library, etc., which Schnyder had so magnanimously put at Froebel's disposal, appeared at first to be all that could be wished. It was most beautifully situated in view of the magnificent chain of the Bernese Oberland, opposite the little town of Sursee, and looking, from different points of view, towards Germany, France, and Italy, as if to indicate its cosmopolitan spirit. It seemed now as if Froebel were about to realise his desire of continuing Pestalozzi's work in the country of the great reformer.

He was gladdened and inspired too by the land in which he was about to sow the seed—the land of beauty, of historic memories, and of freedom; the hills covered with perpetual snow, the mysterious valleys, the blue lakes, the waterfalls, avalanches, precipices, the forests, and the clear bracing air of the hills. Hope and courage once more filled his heart. "Switzerland," says Seyffarth, "is the land of freedom. In lonely valleys or steep mountains, in sunshine or shade, in storm or in calm, everywhere you breathe the breath of freedom. Can we wonder that such a land gave birth to a Wilhelm Tell and a Winkelried?" Such was the spirit in which Froebel began his new work. On the 21st August he and Schnyder signed a contract which in itself is a testimony to the philanthropy and disinterestedness of these two excellent men.*

Schnyder returned to Frankfurt in the beginning of September, leaving a young relative in charge of the Wartensee household, and all promised well. But shortly after the issue of the above-mentioned circular an anonymous article appeared in the Appenzel paper, which made all kinds of unfounded accusations against both Froebel and Schnyder.†

It was headed, "A Word about Friedrich Froebel, of Keilhau, Founder of the Wartensee Institution." Froebel's first impulse was to send to the editor a refutation of the attacks made upon him, but he ended by asking that the article should be signed by the writer, and appealed to the authorities in Rudolstadt, and to the public, to whom he had devoted his life and work, for a thorough investigation. Schnyder, who was much offended by the allusions to him in the offensive publication, urged Froebel from the first to publish an answer which should completely vindicate him and his system, but it was some time before he could win the Keilhau teachers over to this view. At length, however, they consented to draw up a refutation, and one of the Keilhau parents, a man of good position, got the magistrates of Rudolstadt to endorse it. The document was then sent (October, 1832) to the Council of Education at Lucerne. Meanwhile Froebel continued his work in the new institution, and was much appreciated in the neighbourhood. "Many blessed the day that saw his arrival in the canton,

---

* See *Hanschmann*, pp. 222-225.

† This vindictive publication was eventually traced to Froebel's old enemy, Herzog.

and only hoped that the spirit of the institution would spread to other schools."

In January, 1833, a second attack appeared, signed by Dr. Karl Herzog, of Jena. But by this time Froebel had gained friends in Switzerland who were able to testify to the excellence of the school and the integrity and capability of its founders, and several articles in their favour appeared in the *Argau News*. That the school was appreciated is evident from the fact that Froebel was entreated to start others in the neighbourhood. The number of his pupils increased, and he was glad to have the help of his nephew Ferdinand.*

We have a school day at Wartensee described in Froebel's own words: "I am so busy up to three o'clock," he says, "that there is hardly time for breakfast or lunch, and I often work on till late in the night. Lessons begin punctually at eight, although many of the pupils have to come long distances and sometimes through the fiercest weather. After prayers the first lesson is arithmetic, Ferdinand taking one division, I the other; we also share the language teaching that follows. From ten to eleven my nephew gives the upper division a lesson on the history of Switzerland, and the little ones read with me or draw in chequers. This occupation, providing, as it does, exercise in language and training of hand and eye, is both pleasing and good for these Lucerne children. They enjoy their lessons, which not only instruct them but teach them how to live. It was my intention to end the morning school at eleven o'clock, but when the parents saw how the little ones enjoyed their drawing, and how

---

* Son of Christian Froebel.

much they learned from it, they wished the bigger children to learn too; and the only way of getting time for this was to let them stay an hour later. The success of the few who joined at first soon attracted others, and some of them, touched by my 'little magic wand' (the stroke), invent the most beautiful designs.*

"The feeling for art is like a magnet. It soothes the children and keeps them at the table till I break up the class by main force. But mid-day has its duties too, and it is absolutely necessary to dismiss the class a few minutes before noon. One of the boys, who intends to be an artist, will not give up a second of the time, and indeed does all he can to hold on eight or ten minutes longer. After this there is a bare hour before afternoon school (1 p.m.), during which we take our lunch, wash our hands, and do any preparation that may be necessary. The beautiful fruit has often to go away untasted from the table, because there is no time to eat it. The children meanwhile have a good game at catch in the garden until they hear the call to school. By a few minutes past one everything is in order, and we are all quietly at work again. The bigger children do their French exercises, whilst the little ones draw. At two o'clock the little ones write German with me, and the big ones have an oral French lesson. School is over at three. On fine days we have games and gymnastics in the grounds, after which the children disperse. I have

* How different is this description of the Froebel drawing from much of what we know by that name, in which some of the very designs arrived at by Froebel and his pupils whilst applying the principle of harmonising contrasting forms, are worked through by mere imitation.

been much impressed by the refining influence of games for the children. It seems to me that they transform the human being, making many a hard, rough, strong nature gentle and yielding as a plant. Had it been necessary for me to prove the value of the methods adopted at Keilhau, and of their general applicability to human nature, my few weeks' experience with these Swiss children would have been sufficient to convince me. I have watched the effect of our methods every day with increasing satisfaction."

The Wartensee school won, through Schnyder, a friend in the person of Johann Gottlieb Fichte, son of the philosopher who had done so much to befriend Pestalozzi. Young Fichte looked to the Froebel education to work in the direction of his father's doctrines, and determined to do all in his power to spread it. This inspired the Keilhau teachers with the hope that now at length the system would make its way. They had often met Johann Fichte in the merry company of his father's pupils; they knew him to be in earnest, and built much on his support. "Such a test," they write, "of the Froebel idea will show, once for all, whether or not the system forms part of the general scheme of human development. A clear and impartial exposition is most desirable, and it will come better from one who is simply in search of a social and educational reform than from an educational enthusiast, who, however clearly he may see the goal he has in view, is always more or less involved in the struggle to reach it. As for us, let our main concern be to thoroughly test the truth of the fundamental idea rather than to discuss believers and unbelievers in the system, heroes who devote themselves to it, or even the founder of it. What concerns us at present is to encourage all disinterested examination of the question likely to bring out the truth. Let us but seek to know and accept the truth, and act accordingly. Surely it is high time that educated people should be willing to examine a cause that has been publicly advocated as a new development of mankind, and that claims to be a fundamental need of our nation." Young Fichte was much occupied at this time with his own works; but he remained a faithful advocate of Froebel's system of education, and a generation later (*i.e.*, in 1870), in an essay on national education, he justified it from a philosophical point of view.

The Keilhau teachers kept up a good heart even amidst Herzog's persecution of them. "We think," they say, "Herzog's attack may, by drawing attention to the Froebel cause, do good rather than harm. Our little community has grown up like a healthy plant, with a strong root. It is full of life, and grows from stage to stage and from ripeness to ripeness. What we have to do is to stick to our belief, trusting to the truth as our best friend and winner of friends."

Froebel worked most energetically at the new school, but he was greatly in need of more help, and especially of womanly influence. He wrote to Keilhau to see if it were possible for them to spare Ferdinand Froebel's sister Elise to come and mother the Wartensee boys.* After some delay he received their consent, and immediately wrote to Schnyder as follows:—"The difficulties in organising the work of this institution are greater than I expected, and we are greatly in need

---

* Fräulein Salesie, Schnyder's relative, had returned to Lucerne.

of a woman's help. The masculine mind may govern, but it requires the woman's feeling to order and arrange the daily life. For a truly human life in the highest sense both influences are necessary. There are six women workers in Keilhau, each doing her share with dignity, simplicity, and thrift. When the new school was proposed to me, I had these women workers in my mind, but I did not see my way to disturbing the old school for the sake of the new. I know also, from experience, that time alone can bring about a perfect life in any community. I am glad to tell you that I received yesterday the consent of my Keilhau friends to send my niece over here. She has been trained at Keilhau, and can undertake all household matters and help in the school generally. I am sure you feel with me that the sacrifice of so valuable a help shows the great interest the Keilhau teachers take in this new venture, and their harmony of feeling and devotion to the common good. And to judge from your own life, I should say that this is the spirit you would like to encourage at Wartensee." Schnyder fully appreciated the devotion that prompted the Keilhau teachers to deny themselves the services of Barop and Elise Froebel. He, too, felt the need of the woman's influence in the new school, but he thought that so serious a step should only be taken after careful consideration. A good deal of earnest correspondence between Froebel, Schnyder, and Middendorff followed, and in the end Barop was sent over to Wartensee to work with Froebel for a time. With ten dollars (about thirty shillings) in his pocket, he tramped on foot from the heart of Germany to the Sempach Lake, which is not far from Lucerne. Near the end of his journey he made inquiries about the institution, and was informed that the teachers were a company of heretics. This was not encouraging, and Barop began to doubt whether even here, in the land of freedom, Froebel had succeeded in finding the right field for his efforts. A few months later, however, an incident happened which was to give the school a fresh start. Froebel, Middendorff, and Barop were one evening taking rest and refreshment after a walk, at a restaurant in the neighbourhood of Wartensee, and began to discuss the school and the work they had so much at heart. Some merchants from Willisau came in, and, after listening for some time to the eager discussions of the trio, joined in the conversation.

They showed a keen interest in all our friends had to tell them of the aims and objects of the new school, and on their return to Willisau they sent Froebel an invitation to go over there and start a school similar to the one at Wartensee. A small union, consisting of about twenty well-to-do families, guaranteed the necessary funds, and promised to put at their disposal some old Government offices to serve as schoolrooms. Pending the somewhat lengthy negotiations to be gone through before the school could be opened, Froebel went to Keilhau to see his wife and the little community once more. His visit lasted from November till the February of the following year (1833). But, alas! it was much saddened by the loss of his nephew, William,* a most energetic and useful teacher at Keilhau.

On leaving Keilhau, Froebel went to Berlin to see

---

* Ferdinand and William were Christian Froebel's sons.

his mother-in-law. During his stay in the Prussian capital he received a letter from Adolf Frankenberg (the friend and disciple of Krause), which gave him great pleasure. Frankenberg had decided to join the Froebel workers. The Frankenberg family, it will be remembered, were warm disciples of Krause, who had always been their most honoured guest. Frankenberg's father was a man of culture and distinction. He had studied with success both law and finance, but had finally retired to his estate at Eddigehausen, near Göttingen, and his home became the centre of an ideal family and social life. He had five sons, four of whom were gentlemen farmers, and lived in accordance with Krause's principles of sociology. His three daughters* undertook the education of the peasant girls on their estate, whilst their brothers taught the boys. Adolf, the youngest, had finished his studies of philosophy and theology in Göttingen. He was, however, unfortunately prevented from taking his final examination there by the dissolution of the University (1832), and he took for a time a private tutorship. He wanted to perfect himself in method, and to associate with educationists and thinkers; and having a lively recollection of Froebel's visit to Göttingen, and of the interest in his views and principles, he turned to him for guidance. Froebel could not but be gratified at the thought of having a man of such culture and such antecedents to work under him, and on his return to Keilhau gladly carried the good news to his friends, and wrote to assure Frankenberg of a warm welcome amongst the Froebel workers.

* The youngest afterwards went to study under Froebel.

The necessary authorisation for the opening of the new school arrived early in April, and by May 1st Froebel and his wife met Barop, Ferdinand Froebel, and Frankenberg, at Willisau. The school was opened on the following day with thirty-six pupils.

The denser population at Willisau made it more suitable for Froebel's scheme, but, being on the borders of the ultramontane district, it was exposed to the persecution of the Catholic clergy, who from the first had opposed its establishment, and knew well how to stir up opposition against it. Personally there was nothing to say against the "three prophets" (Froebel, his nephew, and Barop), but they were Protestants, and that was enough to awaken alarm in the Catholic mind. The better classes approved of the school and patronised it; but the clergy worked upon the minds of the poor to such an extent that at length there was quite a religious panic, and petitions, appeals, and remonstrances, many with crosses for signatures, began to pour in from all parts of the canton. Barop was especially the object of suspicion, his black coat giving him the appearance of one of the heretic clergy;* and many a battle for principle and right had these noble men to fight, for they were never free from attacks, at meetings, at restaurants, even in the streets. Barop was not actually one of the Willisau staff, but he stuck to his friends, and generally was the one who undertook the defence.

Stopping one day at an inn, on his way to Lucerne, he was pointed at by a priest, who called him "one of the new heretic interlopers." Glances of hatred and

---

* The Protestant pastor was a very pariah in this district.

suspicion were directed towards him. The priest became more and more violent in his denunciations against the "God-forgotten heretic." At last Barop rose slowly, and walking steadily towards his enemy, asked, "Do you know, sir, who Jesus Christ was, and have you any respect for Him?" Confused by the quiet firmness of his manner, the priest answered, "Yes, certainly; he is God's Son, and we must believe in Him and honour Him, unless we wish to be damned eternally." Barop continued, "Perhaps you can tell me whether Christ was a Catholic or a Protestant." The priest remained silent. This question won over the audience, who applauded Barop, and the priest fled.

But the religious persecution thus indicated increased in vindictiveness. The clamour reached the Senate, and though no steps were taken in consequence, the Froebel teachers were warned against the insecurity of their position, and even to avoid lonely rambles over the hills.

Barop relates the following incident:—At the annual church festival in Willisau, it is the custom for the priest to hold up the host covered with spots of blood* as a memorial and warning against evil. All the neighbouring villages assemble and form a procession. Our friends naturally joined, and offered, as their share of the ceremony, to undertake the music. They were not unconscious of the danger of their position, and were prepared to meet any possible attack with firmness and patience. But no sooner had

---

* According to popular belief two gamblers threw javelins at Jesus, whose wounds began to bleed as they exclaimed, "God be with us." The end of the story is that the devil fetched them away.

the music ceased, when a Capuchin monk suddenly appeared upon the scene, and began to rage and gesticulate against the Willisauers for associating with "heretics." The eternal punishment they would suffer for this was described in the most glowing colours, and the people were exhorted to proceed at once against them, "to banish them like wolves from their midst," and so "please God, spite the devil, and win for themselves the blessing of heaven and the approval of God's elect." With the last words the priest vanished through a side door of the church, but not before he had awakened bad feeling amongst the people. Froebel and the teachers stood petrified by the suddenness and violence of the attack, and whilst some of the parents went in pursuit of the priest others closed round the teachers, who were obliged to retire from this dreadful scene amidst the jeers and threats of the crowd. Thenceforth their lives were not safe; indeed, on the following day, as Froebel was starting for a walk, a faithful old Swiss met him with the words, "Don't do it! don't do it! they want to kill you!" "Why?" asked Froebel. The peasant answered, "Custom here—custom here."

At this crisis they thought it wise to apply to the municipality for protection. Barop acted as ambassador, and thus came into contact with the magistrate, Edward Pfyffer, a man of intelligence and education, who gave the following advice:—"There is only one way: that is to win over the people; stick to your work for a little while, and then invite the people from far and near to a public demonstration. If this succeeds you are protected, not otherwise." They followed this plan, and the demonstration took place on a fine autumn day (1833); and as an account of the molestation of the Froebel teachers had been published in several Swiss papers, crowds flocked to Willisau from all the neighbouring cantons, and amongst them even Government delegates from Berne, Zurich, and other towns of more importance. The examination lasted the whole day, ending with games and gymnastics; and, to the delight of the teachers, a complete victory was obtained; the eagerness and simplicity of the children charmed all hearts. They knew that their work was now safe. A public conference was arranged in which Pfyffer, Amrhyn, and other friends and educational authorities took part, and a valiant defence of the Willisauers ensued. A resolution was passed that the building used for the school should be handed over to Froebel at a moderate rent, and the priests who caused the disturbance should be banished the canton.

Having steered the school safely through this difficult crisis, Barop returned to his work at Keilhau. He had been absent over a year, and had not yet seen his little son, now a year old. Middendorff came to Willisau to take his place, bringing Elise Froebel with him, and in his turn leaving wife and children for the work in Switzerland. His support was greatly needed, for in spite of the favourable attitude of the Swiss authorities towards the school and the friendliness of the inhabitants of Willisau, the battle was not yet over. The Catholic clergy did all they could to prevent the school increasing, by prejudicing against it those who were about to send new pupils from a distance. Middendorff stayed on at Willisau for years without visiting his family once. "I did not dare to stir at this time," he said. "I was guarding, as it were, an outpost of our stronghold. As long as the Catholic clergy persisted in their hostilities it was impossible to leave, even for the sake of my dear ones. And yet," he added, smiling, "I can hardly understand now how I did it." It was a peculiarity of Froebel's influence to inspire this unquestioning devotion in his followers. Fellenberg would have liked to win Middendorff for his school at Hofwyl; but Middendorff, who was love and fidelity personified, stuck valiantly to his post. There were other obstacles to be overcome besides the opposition of the Catholic clergy. "It seems to me," writes Froebel, " that education in the canton is more hindered by selfishness and egotism even than by bigotry. The public approve of the education proposed for them, the means are ready to hand, but no one will take the first step. Our public demonstrations have awakened in the minds of the public a desire for the new education; but they act like people who, though they want their cow to give good milk, are unwilling to provide it with good food and shelter."

The Bernese government had, in 1833, shown its confidence in Froebel by sending some young teachers to Willisau to be trained.* In 1835 he was appointed director of a new school which he had been invited to organise in the Orphanage at Burgdorf. Hence, in the summer of that year, he and Langethal settled there with their wives. Middendorff meanwhile took

* One of these writes :—" A teacher such as Froebel is seldom seen. He knew how to stimulate and develop; he would utilise anything that came to hand—number, language, play; all was grist that came to his mill. With little children he was in his element, and they seemed to be quite captivated by his rapid manner and clear demonstration."

Froebel's place at Willisau. There was a training class of sixty students, and the Bernese Government arranged that every teacher in the canton should have three months' leave of absence in the year, so as to be able to attend the Froebel classes and conferences. There was a day school for the children of the town, and a scheme was started for a boarding school for pupils living at a distance. Thus Froebel found himself plunged into manifold difficulties and problems of elementary education, and for a time his scheme for "the education of mankind" had to wait.

In spite of this, he and his wife spent a very happy time at Burgdorf. The lovely valley of the Emme, with its innumerable tributaries, châlets, and watermills, was a constant source of enjoyment to them. The view on every side of this fruitful valley is grand and imposing. Within a few miles on the north-east is a long row of the Jura chain; opposite this, a little further off, are magnificent ice-fields. Just towering with solemn dignity above the little town, you see the majestic peaks of the Bernese Oberland, Schreckhorn and Jungfrau, Eiger and Moench. The view on a clear day, or by a fine sunset, is the grandest and most beautiful that can be imagined; and, to add to its impressiveness, a solitary rock rises from the River Emme, and on its summit stands the Castle of Burgdorf.* It would almost appear that Froebel had reached his goal. Besides being at the head of two thriving institutions, Keilhau (now under Barop) and Willisau (under Middendorff), he held an influential position

---

* Here, on this rock, had the philanthropist, Pestalozzi, laboured in the cause of elementary education, and it was probably within the walls of this old castle that he spent some of his happiest days.

in the most advanced canton of Switzerland. Teachers and pupils alike were devoted to him, and he had the satisfaction of working in a place closely associated with Pestalozzi's labours. The simple, honest, and thrifty life of the Burgdorfers was a source of pure happiness to Froebel; and he began to feel that here, away from persecution and strife, he should be able to carry out the principles which had so long occupied his thoughts.

He had not as yet been able to put into practice the idea which at this time occupied him so much, *i.e.*, the "complete development of the child from within outwards." And the more he studied the question, the more he felt the need of beginning with the earliest years of the child's life, and the more he realised the stupendous difficulties that surround the educator in the school proper. In accordance with his scheme for Helba, he now organised a department for children from three years, who would pass somewhere between four and six into the lowest class of the elementary school. Froebel noted the young child's early observation of his surroundings, and his eagerness to express his understanding of them. He saw that the simple actions, involved in this expression, furnish the young child with the very opportunity he needs, of living out the life that is in him. Expression is life to him.

With this principle in his mind, he would have the young child provided with rhymes, songs and games, objects and materials for manipulation, gymnastic exercises, and simple stories and poems.

Froebel made a study of what is called play. "What is the play of these little ones?" he asks.

"It is the great game of life itself in its beginnings. Hence the intense seriousness often observed in the attitude of children at play." All this naturally led to a reform of family life, to the training of the mother. The home, like the school, must be adapted to the child's development. School training and home training must go hand in hand. Mother and teacher must work towards the same end. These reflections gradually engrossed more and more of Froebel's attention, till at length the idea of the *earliest* training left him no rest. He studied the French crèche system, but this did not, in his opinion, adequately develop the child's powers. What Froebel wanted was a steadily progressive education from first to last. This will only be possible when the mother has learnt how to stimulate the child's powers in such a way that he may grow and flourish "as a plant does under favourable conditions."

Here was the problem, the solution of which led Froebel directly to his Kindergarten; to apply the Pestalozzian principle of Anschauung in such a way as to induce in the child clear and strong impressions, and provide suitable exercises for his moral and spiritual nature. The Anschauung to be followed by a Darstellung, which should bring about a harmonious development of the child. But where begin? Which among his many playthings should be his first object, his first gift? Where is the starting-point? Some children playing at ball in a field gave him the answer. The first gift shall be the ball. It typifies the self-activity of the child, his individuality, and his connectedness with the human race and the universe. Its variety of resource and almost life-like mobility make it a welcome object to the little child. With the ball as outward, and his self-activity as inward means for his development, we have a point of departure which is as perfect as it is simple. That children *self-active* and at *play* with the *ball* should provide the key to his new education, seemed to Froebel an inspiration, almost a revelation.

Froebel believed that a more perfect organisation of family life would inaugurate "a glorious revival; a very renewal of life; a spring-time of humanity; a new era; a millennium." "The family alone," he says, "offers the highest expression of human life, the divine in the human. Life is only complete in the family—father, mother, child. Light, love, and life, are a complete cycle. Only in the sacred soil of the family can the seeds of the new life be sown."* Froebel had some idea at this time of emigrating to America, there to found a Krausean community, and establish his system on the basis of the "new family life."

In a letter to his friend, Adolf Frankenberg, dated Burgdorf, December 31, 1835, he gives a short retrospect of his efforts, which at this point is interesting as part of his history. "After fifteen years' work at Keilhau," he says, "I left it in the care of my three friends. Then I worked at Willisau for three years, one of the same trio taking up my work. Here (at Burgdorf) I have hardly been one year, when I must leave it to another of this faithful trio to continue. Everywhere unity, everywhere trinity—meeting and parting—parting and meeting." Froebel expected in

---

* See an article in the *Sonntagsblatt*, 1838.

this year, 1836, to see the fruition of all his work. The very date was a symbol of good omen to him.*

From a letter of Langethal's, dated February, 1836, we see that from the beginning of his stay in Burgdorf Froebel had been working more and more in the direction of infant education. "I see," he says, "in this new home education of Froebel's both the beginning of all art and science, and the last link in the educational reform that has been going on from Comenius to Pestalozzi and our own times. It is the first rung in the ladder that will lead to truly human family life, and be the best aid to parents. I will do anything to bring it about. I am interested in Switzerland and its industrious and thrifty people, but am willing to work at Keilhau, or anywhere where I am most wanted. I am busy working out some good methods for nature teaching, language and music, and shall want them tested by our little circle at Keilhau."

It was in 1836 that the cube became prominent amongst the gifts. Froebel had language cubes and mathematical cubes. The size was that of the whole third gift. The cube was taken as the typical geometrical form, equally and harmoniously developed on every side. The child was to begin its geometry with a solid, not with the more abstract line as heretofore. The qualities of the cube were to be learned by seeing, handling, observing, verifying, and thus provide a solid basis for the child's geometry. The mathematical

* In a fantastic and fanciful way he reads the date as follows:— Tot up the digits 1, 8, 3, 6, and you get 18—eighteen, achtzehn, achtsen, achtsam, *i.e.*, to be on the watch; or the last two, 3 and 6, and you get 9—nine, neun, neuen, new, renewal. Nine is three times three, *i.e.*, drei mal drei, treu der treu, fidelity; true to *God*, to *nature*, and to *self*.

ideas suggested by the cube were to be verified in the child's life.

The sharp Swiss air does not seem to have agreed with Frau Froebel, who became more and more ailing. With her usual heroism she had, as long as possible, kept this to herself. At length, however, she was overcome by an irresistible longing to visit Keilhau once more, and to see her mother in Berlin. A serious consultation was held, and it was decided that she and Froebel should first go to Berlin, and then to Keilhau to start the new work. Adolf Frankenberg was to join them at Easter. Langethal was to take Froebel's place at Burgdorf, with Sidonie Krause* as mother and manager of the household. Meanwhile, in the middle of March, Frau Froebel received the sad news of her mother's death. This grief added much to her suffering, and the doctor prescribed a return to Germany at the first possible moment.

On his way to Keilhau, Frankenberg visited his friend Leonhardi, and discussed with him Froebel's new plan. Ever since Krause's death (at Munich, in 1832) his friend and disciple, Leonhardi, had been agitating for the publication of his works. He now saw in Froebel's new scheme of education the realisation of the very principles advocated by Krause, and determined to join the Froebelians at once. He wrote to Froebel on the 5th May, saying: "I have thought, heard, and read much of you since we met, and a recent visit from my old friend Adolf Frankenberg has revived in me the long-cherished wish to come into closer relationship with you and your work. Your constant efforts to bring about a more humanising

* Daughter of the philosopher, and the *fiancée* of Dr. Leonhardi.

education have my heartiest sympathy. I can trace in your practice and Krause's theories the same object, *i.e.*, to lay a new and scientific basis for man's education and social life. I see in the scheme shown me by Frankenberg, as well as in the work of your teachers generally, an expression of Krause's fundamental principles of human society. Indeed I am so much impressed with the harmony between you and Krause, that in offering my services I feel I am helping to spread Krause's doctrines. For myself I feel that I shall gain with you that which nothing in my student's life can give me; whilst, on the other hand, my knowledge of science, and the valuable notes in my possession, will enable me to give instruction in many subjects which demand a teacher's whole attention, and can hardly be expected from those who are otherwise occupied. The natural method of investigating scientific facts, advocated by Krause, is not easy for the uninitiated. I rejoice at the chance of seeing the valuable principles, which it cost my dear friend and master so much to discover, expressed in living words and living actions. The proposed publication of his works may do something to make him better known. But you and your friends will do more; and I know of no employment in which my scientific work could be better utilised, nor any which would so pleasurably stimulate my own activity. If you approve, I am ready to throw in my lot with yours; let each of us contribute his particular strength to the common object. Let us unite our efforts in establishing a more natural education for the human being. Let us found a scientific training school for teachers and educators; a university for the new life."

Froebel was, for the moment, too much pre-occupied with his scheme for infant training to be able to consider adequately any plan for a scientific training school for the more advanced stage, to which Leonhardi alluded, but he was entirely in sympathy with Krause's object, and gladly accepted Leonhardi's offer.

Frankenberg sums up as follows the main Krause-Froebelian principle: "The whole is greater than the part; life is more than thought, and the art of living precedes the art of thinking. And just as the human being is more than mere intellect and reason, so is the study of his development higher than the study of logic and philosophy. Science pure and simple, without form or life, is unsatisfactory, and in the same way knowledge apart from action is unsatisfying. Activity lies at the basis of observation; this is seen in the young child, and indeed throughout human life. It is certain that the first human being ate and drank before he philosophised upon it; and the individual goes through the same experience as the race. Family life precedes theories about it. If life in general is to be reformed, to be rendered throughout continuously harmonious, these reforms must begin in the family, from which every social good proceeds." Krause's clear and connected reasoning is published in a form which prevents it being widely known; his philosophy, however, is so exemplified in Froebel's gifts, games, and occupations, as to make it intelligible to all who wish to understand it.

Froebel's work at Willisau was continued by Middendorff and Ferdinand Froebel until 1839, when their places were taken by young Swiss teachers, thoroughly imbued with the Froebel principles. Middendorff returned to Keilhau, Ferdinand Froebel continuing the work till 1841, when he succeeded Langethal at Burgdorf. His excellent work was terminated a few years later by his sudden death. He was deeply regretted. A crowd of sorrowing friends followed him to the grave.

CHAPTER VIII.

THE FIRST KINDERGARTEN.

1836 TO 1843. BLANKENBURG, FRANKFURT, DRESDEN, LEIPZIG.

Origin of the Gifts—First Play School—Publications—Experiments—Blankenburg the Starting-Place—Educational Tour—Froebel's Propaganda—Training of Infant Teachers—Froebel's Personal Influence—Leipzig—Frankenberg's Work in Dresden—Death of Frau Froebel—Froebel's renewed Interest in his Work—Students attracted to the System—Woman's Influence on Early Education—Name for the New Institution—Four-fold Festival—Objects of the New School—Mutter und Kose Lieder.

FROEBEL left Switzerland in the spring of 1836. He had succeeded in establishing his system, in spite of difficulties and persecution, in the cantons of Berne and Lucerne, and even when he left, the community of spirit that existed between the teachers in Switzerland and those in Thuringia remained unbroken. Froebel's first duty on his return to Germany was to settle the affairs of his late mother-in-law. This kept him in Berlin till Michaelmas, and he spent most of his time visiting the *crèches* and infant schools of the city. Though these institutions had been in existence in Germany for a quarter of a century, they had made very little progress in the way of adapting their methods to the nature of little children. Von Tuerck had started a certain number of *crèches* in Berlin in 1833, under the patronage of the widowed Queen Elisabeth of Prussia.

The practice of getting circles of small children together for educational purposes, though new in Germany, had been a custom among the ancients. Children's circles were known to the Greeks in the times of Plato and Aristotle; and the Jews had their Temple schools for them. The best known and the most important of the modern infant schools was that of Pastor Oberlin, at Walbach, Alsace. This school was placed in 1779 under the direction of Oberlin's faithful servant, Luise Scheppler, who, it was said, had a "man's brain and a woman's heart." The weavers' infant school established at New Lanark, Scotland, by James Buchanan, for "songs, games, and discipline," was an immediate outcome of this. It was built and supported by the Scotch philanthropist, Robert Owen. Though there was little attempt at method in it, it provided a certain amount of sense training, and in so far prepared the children for school life.

Lord Brougham's infant schools, scattered throughout England, were supported by the Marquis of Lansdowne, the Duke of Devonshire, the celebrated Wilberforce Macaulay (father of the historian), and others. There was also, as early as 1820, a model school and a training school for teachers in connection. *Crèches* had been established in various places: at Detmold in 1802; at Berlin in 1819, under the protection of the Princess Alexandrine of Prussia; at Wadzeck in 1825; at Stuttgart in 1829; at Sachsenhausen, near Frankfurt-am-Main, in 1832; at Darmstadt in 1834; and at Mannheim and Heidelberg in 1835. These institutions were more or less imperfect, but they had succeeded in drawing the attention of the public to the need of educating infants.

THE FIRST KINDERGARTEN.

Froebel is the discoverer of a rational and psychological system of training little children, and of promoting their all-round development. The means he uses are such as have been in use from time immemorial. Balls, bricks, sticks, paper, songs, games, and simple gymnastics have always occupied little children; but in an unsystematic, casual, and aimless way.

Froebel has managed to put those objects and occupations at the service of little children in a way both to satisfy their instinctive longing for expression and to give them the discipline they require at this age. And in doing this he has given a new impetus to modern education. Since his time the education of the earliest years has become conscious and intelligent instead of haphazard and accidental. It had often been affirmed that education begins at birth, and Pestalozzi had done good work in this direction. But no one before Froebel had organised a continuous and connected system of training equally applicable to young children of all classes and all nations.

Infant schools and *crèches* were a device for the benefit of the very poor, and aimed rather at relieving the mother than at developing the child. *Crèches*, too, were generally put under the care of those who could earn their living in no other way, and who were utterly ignorant of any method adapted to the educational needs of the child, whilst the object of these new infant schools was the development of the child according to his nature.

Froebel drew up, as the basis of his first actual experiment, a complete course of games and occupations, and these were tried at Blankenburg, in some rooms which the mother institution had, not without difficulty, fitted up for the purpose.

Blankenburg, in the Schwarzthal, is one of the most romantic spots in the Thuringian Forest. It lies, half hidden, above Rudolstadt, at some distance from the high road, and within view of the picturesque castle of Greifenstein. Here Froebel opened, in 1837,* what he called "a school for the psychological training of little children by means of play and occupations."

Froebel's little weekly paper, the *Sonntagsblatt*, 1837 to 1840, written mainly by himself, Langethal, Frankenberg, and other friends, became the medium of communication between the different Froebel centres, and helped to spread Froebel's latest ideas with regard to gifts and occupations for the little ones. Froebel writes: "In the very beginnings of life lie the germs of development, and the future of the child depends on the earliest treatment of these germs. It is for us to see that the child develops, from the first, freely and independently, as complete in himself, and yet as a harmonious part of a larger whole. The family is the child's first school. In the atmosphere of family love he follows his self-active instincts. The occupation school is an extended family, in which the child learns consciously to use senses and limbs, and to develop in harmony with his nature, whilst it supplies knowledge and a means often beyond the reach of home training."

In this paper Froebel advocates the complete and harmonious training of the child by the exercise of his self-active, observative, and productive instincts; in short, by means of a perfect "Darstellung" or revelation of his inner self.

* The year of Pestalozzi's death.

THE FIRST KINDERGARTEN. 147

The drift of the articles in this paper may be inferred from the following titles:—"The Child's Self-active Instincts"; "Training in the Family"; "Educational Family Circles"; "Psychology and School Systems"; "The meaning of the Froebel Gifts and Occupations." Froebel adopted for this paper Goethe's motto, "Come let us live for our children," and, in point of fact, devoted the paper to the solution of the problem of carrying out the principle implied in it. In it he proposes to establish institutions for the complete self-education of the human being by means of spontaneous play and productive activity, for the reorganisation of family life, and the co-operative training of infants.

In September, 1838, Barop and Frankenberg took a few of the Keilhau pupils for a holiday to Dresden, and took with them such of the gifts as were ready (probably Gifts i.–iv.). They called on Prof. Peters at Vitzthum, to whom they had letters of introduction. Frankenberg at once pulled out of his wallet the little boxes he had with him, and began to play with the doctor's two little daughters. After watching the proceedings for some little time the doctor exclaimed, "You must stay here and play with the children; such a gift as you have for teaching is seldom seen; there is meaning in these little games."

From Dresden the friends went to Leipzig and other towns; and Frankenberg gives the following account of the tour to his friend Leonhardi:—"All lovers of children," he says, "are delighted with Froebel's little boxes (the gifts). Dr. Peters, of Dresden, kept all I had. I played with his two little girls. I am told 'they are usually very shy with strangers, especially the elder, who is but five years old.' But they soon got over this on seeing the fourth gift, and cried out, every time I built anything, 'Now let me do it.' Indeed both parents and children were so intensely interested in the gift, that we were occupied with it over two hours, and the children missed their walk.* Dr. Peters wants the complete set. I explained Froebel's theory of the gifts. He and his wife entreated me to stay with them or come back soon, and they said that if Froebel or I would settle here, they would introduce us to many nice people, and we should have plenty to do. They are deeply sensible of the need for training before the school age, and would rejoice to see an institution for this purpose in Dresden. I believe with them that the introduction of the gifts into a city of such educational standing would be a great success. Dr. Peters introduced me to Herrn Director Blochmann, who clearly sees the value of the earliest education, and of a thorough training for those who undertake it. He, too, wants Froebel to come to Dresden and give a course of lectures on the gifts, and is sure they would be well attended. I told him that this was quite possible, and that it had been done at Göttingen with great success. Professor Löwe, Teacher of Mathematics and Ancient Languages, who took such a lively interest in what he saw at Keilhau, laid great stress upon instilling into women the spirit of this education, and wants the mistress of an infant school, whom he knows, to go and study at Blankenburg. I left him a copy of the *Sonntagsblatt*. Gefell, too, a great

---

* Simple demonstrations of this kind do much for the Froebel cause, and should always accompany lectures on the system.

THE FIRST KINDERGARTEN. 149

educationist, is so much impressed with the need of occupying little children, that, in addition to his school work, he has established a self-supporting occupation school for the poor. He asked me to leave him the *Sonntagsblatt* so that he might show it to the Pedagogic Union (an association of the chief professors in Dresden). He said the paper admirably represented modern thought, and he proposed issuing a circular to get subscribers. In short, those who have experience in Dresden are convinced that the cause would succeed here, and entreat the leaders, especially Froebel, to come and start a school. I have promised that one of us will come as soon as possible."

Frankenberg continues: "We next went to Leipzig, where the idea had already been introduced by Langethal. Kaiser, the rector of the school for the deaf and dumb, showed us his system of teaching. He has an excellent school with sixty pupils; he was delighted with our little boxes, and decided to have them. We have his heartiest sympathy. Lindner was much pre-occupied with his own views on religious teaching, but consented after a time to look into the thing, and finally gave his approval. Vogel (a Thuringian), the director of the two middle-class schools in Leipzig, showed us great attention. He sees the value of this training for the little ones; but he says Froebel's apparatus is so simple that it wants demonstrating, and that this was excellently done by Langethal. He went with us to call on Doerffling, the publisher, and ordered a complete set of apparatus for his school, and said he would write a notice of it for the papers.

"I had a long conversation with Doerffling, who highly approves of the boxes, and praises the connectedness of the series. He says that if their use could be clearly demonstrated, Leipzig is the very place in which such an idea would spread. One of us, he says, must come at once. He wants to republish the articles I brought with me upon the second gift. He has sent the gifts to all the chief publishers in Germany. The last thing he said was, that so good a cause, in the hands of such excellent men, is sure to make its way. At Eisenberg, Krause's birthplace, we were welcomed heartily by Herr Klein, who has been a teacher for seventeen years. He thought it admirable that men of our standing should be willing to band themselves together as pioneers of education for the earliest years. He himself is persuaded of the importance of this early training. And I must not forget to mention something I heard in Dresden, which shows that the idea that fills our own minds is working in other regions, where we might perhaps least expect it. A philanthropic Hungarian lady, who has travelled much in Germany in the interests of early education, has finally established in Hungary a training school for young people willing to devote themselves to little children, and this school is well attended.* The conclusions I have come to at the end of my travels are—firstly, that there is a pretty general demand for a more natural, practical, and rational treatment of young children; and secondly, that this treatment demands the services of men

---

* Frankenberg probably means the Countess of Brunswick, who started a training school for teachers at Pesth, where a marble statue has been erected to her memory.

and women of culture, willing to devote their best thought to it, and able to inspire others."

A short extract from a Swiss paper, the *Eidgenosse*, for August, 1838, may be a suitable addition to Frankenberg's account of the Froebel propaganda at this time. It runs as follows:—

"We have already had occasion in these pages to speak of Froebel's work in connection with early education. I would like to draw attention to a new service which he is rendering to the public, *i.e.*, the organisation of the training for little children, which shall harmonise the home and the school. A task implying so many difficulties could only be undertaken by one who, like Froebel, is a genuine lover of children. He has the faith which removes mountains, and which refuses to see anything but the good and the true. In an earlier number of this paper we published an article on 'The First Gift: by Friedrich Froebel.' We now have his second gift (consisting of cube and cylinder), with a very clear and practical guide for its use. Froebel shows by this series of boxes* how well he understands children, and how well he knows how to stimulate their intelligence and interest without overtaxing their powers. We can highly recommend these gifts, as well as the magazine, the *Sonntagsblatt*, to every parent and teacher, and, indeed, to all who are interested in early education, being persuaded that anyone who gives the little boxes a fair trial will see how well suited they are to the nature and requirements of young children."

Meanwhile the friends continued their propaganda zealously. Froebel gave some demonstrations at Göttingen and Frankfurt, whilst Langethal went to Leipzig, whence he wrote: "I am more than ever interested in our work; I had a natural love for it

* First four gifts.

before, but now I think I have a spiritual love for it." Dr. Leonhardi, who had a prominent position in the educational world, and who was well known both at Frankfurt and Darmstadt, won many friends for the new movement. He founded a little society which sent several teachers to Blankenburg to be trained.

Froebel wrote to Leonhardi in September, 1838: "I agree with you that there is a great need both for *infant* training and for *mother* training in the upper grades of society. A couple of hours a day devoted to the children in this way would have an excellent effect upon family life. In the current number of the *Sonntagsbatt* I have suggested small private family circles or unions.* Schaefer has great hopes of the Frankfurt Women's Union. He looks to women to bring about a true regeneration of family life and of society. The fear expressed by some that these institutions will loosen the bond between mother and child, is due to misconception. On the contrary, mothers will have opportunities of seeing their little children at work, and will learn to share their play and occupations, and thus gain much that will help them at home. The intercourse brought about between different families will promote the discussion of educational questions, and this will tend to raise the whole standard of life. Thus you see, dear Leonhardi, that your work for us has for its object the realisation of Krause's ideal. I am ready to comply with your wish as regards the training courses for teachers at Blankenburg; we want a short course for young men with a good education, and a longer

* How much might be done by small unions of mothers co-operating thus for the benefit of their children.

one for those of less experience and less maturity.*
I should like to begin with men of culture, say with
half-a-dozen Langethals. With such men as teachers,
we might hope, in five or ten years' time, to do much
for early childhood. I rejoice in what you tell me of
yourself; you have penetrated into many of the secrets
of childhood, and of those who should have to do
with them. I approve of your proposition to establish
classes for demonstrating the right treatment of young
children, both to teachers and to the elder daughters
in families; but this would be easier far in a large
town like Frankfurt than either at Keilhau or
Blankenburg; and I will do my best, at all events
in the beginning, to give the classes myself. In
short, I am open to any proposition to awaken interest
among women, and to lay a solid foundation for the
education of infants. Only make it possible for me;
give me the soil, and I will thankfully till it; give
me material, and I will shape it. I am glad that you
have renounced the idea of a training school for
teachers in connection with those already in existence,
as I am persuaded this would involve us in so much
conflict and strife that we should be in danger of
losing sight of our object. My ideas could be perfectly well carried out with moderate numbers and
moderate expenditure. It is the simplest possible
plan for training *youths* and maidens for the right
treatment of infancy. What I want especially to teach
them, is how to develop the love of activity that children
show between their *first* and *sixth or seventh years*."†

* It is evident that the first Kindergarten students consisted of men as well as women.

† It is this instinct which runs to seed and causes "naughtiness," if unutilised.

Froebel had set up, in what he called his "workshop," a small printing press, by means of which he prepared the articles on the gifts which appeared in the *Sonntagsblatt*. One of his former pupils, a painter, named Unger, undertook to lithograph the illustrations for him,* and many a busy hour did they spend together in "the office."

The children's institution at Blankenburg† attracted many visitors, amongst the most frequent of whom were Caroline Louise, Dowager Duchess of Schwarzburg-Rudolstadt, and her sister, the Princess of Schaumberg-Lippe. The Princess Ida was known in the neighbourhood as "the children's friend." Many other visitors came. Anyone passing through Thuringia with any pretension to a knowledge of education, made a point of seeing the wonderful friend of little children.

In the autumn of 1838, a Dr. Stoy,‡ principal of a boys' school at Jena, spent a few days at Blankenburg, and appeared to be much interested in Froebel's occupations for children. Another of the visitors, Professor Schmidt (Principal of the Agricultural and Technical School at Straubingen), succeeded in bringing the new institution to the notice of some distinguished men in Munich. Deinhard, another of the visitors, says: "I had hardly settled in Blankenburg when a tall, lean, active-looking man called upon me, bringing with him a quantity of apparatus, which he placed upon our tables and bureaus, coming as often as possible to

---

* Unger later on illustrated the *Mutter-und Kose-Lieder*.

† The name Kindergarten had not yet been found.

‡ Dr. Stoy, author of a handbook of occupations for young boys, was at this time studying in Göttingen under Herbart (reappointed since 1833).

demonstrate with them. The least show of interest would fill him with delight and enthusiasm. In every fresh visitor he saw the promise of fruitful soil in which to sow his seed. He was full of ideals and plans for human happiness, and his enthusiasm and energy were extraordinary. I did not at first understand his ideas; but I appreciated then, as now, the dignity of his aim, and I could clearly trace his devotion to his work, and his love of humanity in every word he uttered; and his rapidity of thought and eloquence were both fascinating and inspiring."

In January, 1839, Froebel, with Middendorff and Adolf Frankenberg, went to Dresden, where one of his "Play Schools" was opened. There was a large gathering, and he gave an excellent lecture, explaining the principles and methods to be adopted, and showing that in supporting a system which treated young children properly, Dresden would be working for the good of all humanity. He dwelt upon the necessity of following the laws of nature in education. He showed and explained his series of playthings, starting with the ball. The lecture was largely attended by all grades of society, including the Queen of Saxony.

The Queen showed much interest both in the lecture and in the little lesson which Froebel gave to some young girls, and he was asked to repeat his demonstration before a society of savants. The whole series of gifts and occupations were shown, including drawing, painting, and maps; and they declared the system to be pre-eminently logical and practical. It provided training for hand and eye, for the imagination and taste; and was altogether stimulative and bracing. Principal Otto expressed his keen appreciation of the teaching, and his amazement at Froebel's energy and enthusiasm.* He said he was like an inexhaustible mine of precious metals. He took Froebel and Frankenberg to see a *crèche* in which he was interested, and to his and the children's great delight Frankenberg attended daily for some weeks, in order to give illustrations of games and occupations. Many visitors went to see this and to talk with Froebel.

A committee was formed, consisting of professors and others distinguished for their social or educational position. They discussed the establishment of a Froebel Institution for Dresden, with Frankenberg as director; also the modification of school organisation, with a view to introducing Froebel's gifts and occupations.

A young Pole, Theophil Nowosielsky, who had come to Dresden at this time to enquire into infant-school systems, was much attracted by Froebel's ideas. This young man hoped to bring about an association between the Thuringian teachers and the society he represented at Warsaw, and to be the means of introducing the system into Poland. "I cannot understand," he said to Froebel, "how anyone can fail to see the extreme value of your system, with its delightful sequence and order."

Froebel and Middendorff next went to Leipzig to see the editor of the *Sonntagsblatt*, leaving Frankenberg in Dresden. Here they lectured to mixed audiences, with the result that Froebel was invited to send in plans for the establishment of an infant school in the town. Doctor Vogel, the Director of the High School in which

* "The ideas possess Froebel rather than he them," said Luise Frankenberg.

the lectures were held, expressed the highest approval of Froebel's efforts. "This development of education downwards, towards the beginnings," he said, "is exactly what we want." Vogel's zealous advocacy of the system not only made many converts in Leipzig, but reacted favourably upon the more conservative Dresdeners. Whilst the preliminaries were going on for the establishment of a play school in Dresden, Frankenberg occupied himself in a private room with a few children of the well-to-do classes. After a time Professor Loewe gave him the use of a house at the seaside with a large garden attached, and here he taught as many as forty children at a time. Froebel rather hoped Dresden would become a propaganding centre for the system. In this he was disappointed, but the spark kindled there by Frankenberg has not died out.*

On his return to Blankenburg in April, Froebel found his wife very seriously ill. Frau Froebel was the author of many a little song and rhyme for Kindergarten children, and though childless herself, proved a very spiritual mother to the little crowd for whom her husband so zealously worked. She had from the first given herself whole-heartedly to the Froebel cause, and thoroughly understood it. She expresses her sense of its value in the following simple little verse:

> "Ein leichter Sinn der fasst es nicht,
> Ein leiser Sinn der hasst es nicht;
> Ein lauter Sinn verspottet's nur,
> Ein tiefer folgt allein der Spur."†

---

* For an account of the origin of the Kindergarten in Dresden, see the *Erziehung der Gegenwart* for 1874.

† "The superficial grasp it not,
The rough and coarse can only sneer;
It wants the thought of gentle minds
To grasp its meaning true and clear."

She lost her foster-daughter in the beginning of May, and did not survive her many days. Possibly grief may have hastened her death. She died on the 13th May, aged fifty-nine. Although she had been ailing so long, her death was a terrible blow to Froebel. She had prevented Middendorff from sending Froebel the bad news of her failing health to Dresden, although she felt that no one nursed her so well as her husband. She was buried at Blankenburg on the 17th May, 1839.

Middendorff wrote to Leonhardi a few days after her death:—"Frau Froebel passed gently away on Monday, 13th May. I came over in the afternoon, and she recognised me, and asked after the teachers and children at Keilhau. To the last she interested herself in the education of the little ones. I have known many noble women, but none nobler. She lived for the happiness, the enfranchisement, and the good of mankind." Middendorff carried Froebel off to Keilhau for a time, hoping that the new infant education going on there would divert his thoughts from his sorrow.

The grief caused by the illness and death of Frau Froebel interrupted the publication of the *Sonntagsblatt*, and it was only in 1840 that Froebel picked it up again. He writes: "Since my great sorrow, it has been very hard for me to recommence my work. In my wife I have lost the most sympathetic companion, and the cause the most faithful friend. Her devotion to the welfare of little children was untiring, and it is only amongst the children she loved so well that I have been able to find my life again. The happiness of the little ones at Keilhau, the fidelity of my friends, the approval of the authorities, and the interest of the students in my work, have all helped to rekindle within me the life which she so heartily shared."

Froebel returned to Blankenburg in June; a distant relative undertook the housekeeping for him. He began at once teaching his occupations and games to large classes of thirty and forty children, whose ages varied from one to seven years. Elder brothers and sisters, and even mothers, often asked to share these lessons.

That he was utterly absorbed in his new work is evident from his words to Dr. Ruete: "The children," he writes, in October, "are treated according to their individuality, and develop freely and naturally in body and mind. The system stimulates their reason and their sense of order and beauty. They enter zealously and heartily into the spirit of the work. Nothing is done for show; everything for the development of the 'highest in life.'" In the late autumn Froebel undertook several courses of training, which were attended by teachers of good educational standing. Amongst these were Dr. Weil, who joined with the intention of introducing the system into his father's school; and Herr Hochstaedter, whose object was to start a Froebel infant school for the Jews in Frankfurt. Early in 1840 Karl Schneider came from Frankfurt, and Dr. Kern from Eisenach. The latter applied Froebel's methods to the teaching of the deaf and dumb. Froebel's great wish at this time was to form a union of women teachers throughout Germany, and to make the institution at Blankenburg serve both as a pattern to teachers and a centre for their training. He hoped that all Germany would come to sympathise with his object. He wrote to the Duchess of Schwarzburg-Rudolstadt, proposing to make the following Christmas the occasion for starting a National Women's Union for child culture. He says: "The more I study childhood, the more I am persuaded of the importance of this period of life for the future of the human being, and the more clearly do I see the need for the co-operation of intelligent women in the education of the young. It is during these earliest years that the seeds of virtue and goodness are sown, and the basis of a happy human life is laid.

"Womanly love, as well as manly strength, are necessary for the child's perfect development. Women of the middle classes do little for the all-sided and highest life of their children; and women of the lower classes do a great deal less. What we want is a band of earnest, noble-minded women who will form a national association for the benefit of infancy. Their object should be to surround children with the conditions favourable for a perfect education, and to avert from them everything that threatens to hinder and spoil it. This will develop the best qualities in the heart of man, and purify and ennoble human life. Whatever has to be done for the human being should be done in his earliest years, and that persistently. Intermittent and casual training is of little service. Under present conditions there is a great deal to undo before we can train a child as it should be trained, and make it amenable to good influences. We want the practical help of motherly women, and this we shall only get when our girls are trained to understand childhood."

THE FIRST KINDERGARTEN.

"Dir vertraue ich mein Heil'ges an, die Keime der Schöpfung,
Deiner Pflege die kommende glückliche Nachwelt.
Ehret die Frauen, ihr Nam' ist Befreiung. Anfang und Ende
  Stehet in einem Blick ihnen da! Auch Wege zum Ausgang—
Schaut Ariadnens Krone, ihr Retterinnen, und reichet,
Reichet den Faden der Labyrinth verirreten Menschheit.
  Sinn't und erziehet (Ihr könnt es allein) die glückliche
    Nachwelt."—HERDER.

Froebel had for some time been in search of a name for his new movement. "Ah!" he would exclaim, "how I wish I could find a name for my youngest born!" And one fine summer day (1840), walking over the hills towards Blankenburg with Middendorff and Barop, suddenly he stopped and shouted joyfully, "Eureka, I have found it! 'Kindergarten' is the word." He had at length found a name he liked for his new institution. The next thing was to arrange for a christening, which should introduce the new name to the public. It had been customary at Keilhau to celebrate each pupil's birthday. But as the number of pupils increased, and this became difficult, it was agreed that some particular date should be chosen to serve as a general birthday. Now the teachers thought of having the christening of the institution on the same date; and to add to the solemnity and festivity of it, they selected the 28th June (1840), which was the four-hundredth anniversary of Gutenberg's invention of printing. Thus a four-fold celebration was decided upon; for the 28th June was the midsummer holiday as well. It happened to be a most beautiful day. Keilhau and Blankenburg, the mother and daughter institutions, vied with each other in adding to its happiness and success, and showed more clearly than ever how closely and harmoniously they worked together. Indeed, they made the impression of a single institution for the training of childhood and youth. At break of day pupils and teachers met on the Dessau,* and formed a procession, which wound its way, amidst singing and rejoicing, towards Keilhau, where the first part of the proceedings was to take place. They stopped to see the sun rise. Froebel said it was like Gutenberg holding the torch of enlightenment over the world; and as the sun broke through the clouds he said, "That is how our new work will have to break through darkness and difficulty; just as the mind itself has to win its way to light and truth."

They reached the school about six o'clock. The first thing they did was to celebrate the general birthday. Middendorff delivered the birthday address, which led in a natural way to the birth of the Kindergarten, and the new life for mankind it was to inaugurate.

Hymns were sung, and greetings exchanged; then came breakfast, after which they climbed the Spizberg, to reach the friendly little church of Eichfeld. Here a sermon was preached by one of the Keilhau teachers, the text being, "There are many gifts, but one spirit." To this peaceful morning succeeded a merry afternoon, when all started for Blankenburg, where the second part of the proceedings was to take place. Wagonettes, decorated with green branches and flowers, filled with pupils, teachers, girls and women, all singing songs applicable to the occasion, went down through the beautiful valley of the Saal. As they passed through

---

* A mountain to the south of Keilhau.

Volkstaedt and Schwarza, they were greeted with cheers and hurrahs. Undismayed by occasional showers of rain, they reached Blankenburg, and in the market-place struck up a song in honour of the town.

"Schaut hier die Stadt, gelegen schon,
 Von grünen Bergen schön umspannt,
Die hoch die alte Burg lässt sehn,
 Wo Kaiser Gunthers Wiege stand.
Gegrüsset sei uns diese Stadt,
 Die schützend Kinderpflege hat.

Schaut hier die Stadt im Flurengrün
 Von Fleiss und Fruchtbarkeit erfüllt,
Die Rinn und Schwarza schön umziehn,
 Wo Wasser der Genesung quillt,
Gegrüsset sei uns diese Stadt,
 Die schützend Kinderpflege hat.

Schaut hier die Stadt, wo keimt und blüht,
 Was Viele lange schon ersehn,
Das unsre Schaar auch hierher zieht,—
 Ein Kindergarten im Entstehn.
Gegrüsset sei uns diese Stadt,
 Die schützend Kinderpflege hat.

Heil dir, du Stadt, ob klein, doch gross,
 Bist stark und edel du gesinnt,
Und nährest treu in deinem Schoss
 Das dir vertraute deutsche Kind.
Wir Wollen all' dir Liebe weihn,
 Und stimmen gern zum Preise ein."

The Gutenberg festival was celebrated in the new Town Hall. The Keilhau Choir, assisted by some singers from Rudolstadt, sang Doering's "Bergman's Gruss," a most suitable performance for the occasion. It seemed to speak Froebel's message. "Rejoice, rejoice," he cried, as he described the difficulties that had preceded the triumph of the wonderful but simple invention; and he showed how valuable was the printing-press, and what a debt humanity owed to it; how it was the means of uniting all nations and all times, past, present, and future. He next went on to speak of the new education under women, and of the proposed association for the training of infancy, to be called the "German Kindergarten Association." He then addressed himself more especially to the women in his audience: "Do not be afraid to start on this work," he said; "make a beginning, however small. Every good thing has had its origin in the imperceptible. How often what appears to be dead and hidden is brought back to life by the warmth of the spring sun. Only have faith, and you will win for your nation and for humanity a regeneration of child-life. This can only be brought about when the truth about childhood has sunk deep into the heart of the nation.

"Do not deceive yourselves; let no one persuade you that women are not concerned in the well-being of mankind. Women's unions are always successful: look at the *Crèche* Union. Open your hearts; the spirit of the undertaking I advocate is far more clearly written there than in my explanation. Childhood, like spring-time, is very fleeting; but surely the beautiful is no less beautiful because it is transitory, nor the good less good because you can only feel it in your heart. It is the right, the true, the good, and the beautiful that ennoble our life. Melody and song are no less a gift than metal which we can feel with our hands. A real joy for the child, as well as for the educator, lies in the simple, natural stimulation of his instinct for self-activity."

THE FIRST KINDERGARTEN.

Immediately after Froebel's address the Blankenburg Kindergarten children appeared as if by magic, and began to play some of their games, thus giving a living demonstration of happy natural development. Meanwhile, in a side room, the signatures of those who wished to join the new Kindergarten Union were taken. Parents, teachers, nurses, and friends of little children were all invited to join, and form one educational body. The union was to have a training and practising school for male and female teachers; a perfectly-fitted model school for children; and a journal of its own. The training was to include all kinds of needlework and house duties. It was calculated that a capital of fifteen thousand pounds (to be raised by shares of thirty shillings each) would be needed for a suitable building in Blankenburg. Froebel hoped for a sufficient response to his appeal to German women to be able to start at once. But the time was not yet ripe. Wichard Lange says: "Froebel had no worldly wisdom; but the world wants such men as he to scatter seeds and keep up its ideals." The institution, though for a time it existed but in thought, was not forgotten. The following passage appeared the next year in the *National Advertiser*, under the heading, "The Blankenburg Kindergarten and Institution for the Training of Infant Teachers."

"We have," it said, "urgent need of an institution for the training of nurses and teachers of young children. This is of more importance than schools, academies, universities, or any other educational institutions, because it would enable us to send forth the young from their nurseries healthy in mind and body, with pure and sensitive hearts, prepared for educational influences."

"It is surprising," it went on, "to see the order and harmony that reigns amongst these little citizens under six years of age. The very smallest of them evidently feels himself to be a responsible member of the little community; and far from wishing by frivolity, or perversity, to disturb the order of the class, he responds readily to the gentle discipline that rules and directs the proceedings, and is delighted to lend his small powers to the completion of the common task. It is interesting to watch the children's pleasure as they feel the ball quickening under their hands, or build some simple object with their bricks, or in some other way represent the familiar scenes and doings of ordinary life, such as feeding chickens, raking, mowing, digging, or hammering. The Kindergarten games lend themselves charmingly to these little dramas."

Children from Rudolstadt often took part in these doings, and soon there was a flourishing Kindergarten for the higher classes. Many women and young men interested in infant education, or destined to be directors of middle-class Kindergartens, came to Blankenburg to be trained. On Sunday afternoons the children came from the neighbouring villages, and Froebel and Middendorff invented songs, rhymes, and occupations for them.

The well-known *Mutter-und Kose-Lieder*, bearing the somewhat bulky title, "A Family Book for Developing the Self-activity of Childhood," was printed by Froebel at Blankenburg in 1843.

It had taken many years to prepare for publication. It contains fifty little songs or games, with illustrations and explanatory mottoes. The rhymes are here and there somewhat stiff and stilted, and the illustrations not always perfect as works of art, especially as regards the figures and faces. But the book is unique as the expression of motherly feeling and spiritual truth. There is hardly a superfluous line in the drawings or an accidental word in the songs. Everything follows an educational sequence, which is explained in the mottoes at the top of each page. It is both a book for mothers and a mothers' book, *i.e.*, it serves as a guide for the mother, and is in harmony with her instincts. It shows how the mother, by her love, develops tenderness in the child; and it gives her things to do of which she best knows the value.

> "Was sinning die Mutter wecket und pfleget
> Mit heiterernstem Spiele und Lied ;
> Was ihre Liebe schützend umheget
> Wirkt segnend fort bis ins tausendste Glied."*
> Innig sich verschiedenes verbindet
> Und Getrenntes sich in Ein'gung findet ;
> Eins dem Andern zur Entwicklung nützt,
> Eins das Andre helfend unterstützt ;
> Drum—in Allen wirkt und schafft Ein Leben,
> Weil das Leben all'ein ein'ger Gott gegeben.†

The united family life at Keilhau gave Froebel plenty of opportunity for observing the characteristics of childhood, and Frau Froebel, in her loving, cosy way, had tried most of the gifts, games, and occupations upon Middendorff's bright and healthy children. Two of these were general favourites—little Alwina and the

---

* The love evoked in the infant mind
  By the mother's gentle voice and song
 Remains and grows, and leaves behind
  That which endures the whole life long.—*Tr.*

† In the varied world of nature,
   'Midst contrasting forms of life,
   Underlies a bond of union,
   Peace amidst apparent strife.
   All things ever intertwine,
   Bounded by the law divine.—*Tr.*

eldest boy. Froebel had put much of his experience of childhood into his *Education of Man*. In his *Mothers' Book* he endeavoured to perpetuate and further develop the playful ways of little children on the one hand and the mothers' methods on the other. He dedicated the book to the memory of his wife.* Many more elaborate games have been published since the mother songs, but none more closely exemplify the interrelation of mother and child. It was one of the mothers at Keilhau who gave Froebel the first idea for these infant games and songs. Carrying her baby round the farmyard, she taught it to beckon to the animals and call to them in an encouraging tone of voice. "Chuck, chuck, chuck," she said, "call the chickens." "Roocoo, roocoo, roocoo, little pigeon."

Froebel took note of this, and he and his wife made their first little infant game with it. The book shows how the child proceeds from the outward form of things to their inner meaning. The little child begins by perceiving and realising his surroundings. Next he learns to *look for* and *observe* them, and at last he is able to form a conception of them, and to show this by Darstellung, or giving out that which he has taken in. If the first step be missing the succeeding ones are impossible.

Froebel calls the book a starting-point for a healthy and natural education. Frau von Marenholtz says: "Only those who have forgotten their own childhood, and are ignorant of child-nature, can disdain this attempt to foster and stimulate the first signs of mental and spiritual life. There is an unbroken continuity from the first lisping of infancy to the wise

* It was published in 1843, four years after her death.

words of the sage; and if we want perfectly developed human beings, capable of realising the ideals of youth, we must learn to regard education as a continuous whole, as a unity too sacred to be broken or interfered with."*

"Sharp limits and definite subdivisions within the continuous series of the years of development, withdrawing from attention the permanent continuity, the living connection, the inner living essence, are highly pernicious, and even destructive in their influence. Thus it is highly pernicious to consider the child or boy as something wholly different from the youth or man, and as something so distinct that the common foundation (human being) is seen but vaguely in the idea and word, and scarcely at all considered in life and for life.

"And yet this is the actual condition of affairs. The youth no longer sees in himself the boy and the child—with affected superiority he scorns them. It is possible only to indicate, but not to point out in their full extent, the unspeakable mischief, disturbance, and hindrance in the development and advancement of the human race arising from these divisions and limitations. This disregard of the value of earlier—and particularly of the earliest—stages of development with reference to later ones prepares for the future teacher and educator of the boy difficulties which it will be scarcely possible to overcome. How different would this be in every respect if parents were to view and treat the child with reference to all stages of development and age, without breaks and omissions; if, particularly, they were to consider the fact that the vigorous and complete development and cultivation of each successive stage depends on the vigorous, complete, and characteristic development of each and all preceding stages of life. The child, the boy, man, indeed, should know no other endeavour but to be at every stage of development wholly what this stage calls for."—From HAILMANN's Translation of *The Education of Man*, § 22.

* *Child and Child-nature.*

CHAPTER IX.

THE FROEBEL PROPAGANDA IN GERMANY AND BELGIUM.

1843 TO 1849. DARMSTADT, LEIPZIG, DRESDEN.

The Froebel Community—Letter to Leonhardi—Professor Ahren's—Development of Kindergarten Apparatus—Foelsing—Kindergarten Games—New Societies—Difficulties at Blankenburg—Frankenberg—Froebel in Saxony—Kindergarten Conference—Middendorff's Address—Froebel in Dresden—Marquart—The Baroness of Marenholz Bülow.

FROEBEL was pretty well known in the North of Germany by the end of the year 1842. The Blankenburg teachers had started Froebel schools at Gerau, Hildburghausen, Coburg, and Sondershausen; whilst at Rudolstadt a Kindergarten for the upper classes was opened under the patronage of the Dowager Duchess.

A beautiful building with covered playground had been obtained for it, and six ladies took it in turns to assist the Kindergarten teacher, the Princess Caroline of Schaumburg-Lippe being one of the most active.*
Frau Kern, too, who had studied Froebel's system at Blankenburg, now used it in the institution for the deaf and dumb at Eisenach, of which her husband was the principal. Teachers came from various parts of Germany to learn the system. In Hungary the Kinder-

* How good it would be if well-to-do families in England would unite into Kindergarten circles, the mothers assisting to teach by turns.

garten was by this time acknowledged to be a necessary part of national education, and several young Hungarian teachers came to Blankenburg to study the system.

The following extract from a letter Froebel wrote to his friend Leonhardi will show that progress was also being made in Belgium: "I am much interested in Ahren's report of children's doings in Brussels. You seem to have developed in Belgium in a natural way what we are striving to establish in Germany scientifically. I wish every nation would learn to care for its children. This would do more than anything else to rid our own children of what you call 'German intellectual clumsiness.' I agree with you that it is good for the little ones to have the sympathy and supervision of elder brothers and sisters in their play. As for my part in the movement, I am but the mouthpiece of an idea, which sooner or later is sure to make itself felt. These games and occupations find acceptance with all grades of children, and are welcome in sickness and in health. And often children who are weary of their more elaborate playthings, will turn to my simple gifts with renewed pleasure. I am persuaded that a clear perception of their meaning will be a blessing for present and future generations. Modern education does not tend to fit the human being for the highest life he can lead. In the hurry of school business he gets no opportunity for the training of his powers, nor for the consideration of ideas from different points of view, which is the only way to make them his own. He has too little chance of fulfilling the divine exhortation to be perfect, 'as your Father in heaven is perfect.'

"There is a certain course and sequence in the development of all things, which the Creator has followed in building up the race, and which the human being must be allowed to follow if he is ever to approach perfection. This course is open to every creature, no matter what the stage of his development may be. We must start right. It is hopeless to try and win for a creature already developed the freshness, freedom, happy spontaneity, and energy which characterise a natural development."

In 1843 Froebel published a short account of "The Kindergarten in Germany," and Myer, the publisher at Hildburghausen, wrote an introduction, in which he says: "In the Kindergarten we have the spring-time of the nation, the blossom of eternity. In caring for children we are doing our best for our country. Children are the bond between the past and the future. It must be the interest of all of us to cultivate the child garden, and to make it good and beautiful. The Kindergarten appeals to the heart of every parent. May its founder find many followers, and may he live to see his efforts crowned by the establishment of thousands of Kindergartens." Karl Schneider, too, had published the year before a favourable view of the system in his *Creation, the Creator, and the Natural Law*. But in spite of the approval of educated men, the movement advanced but slowly, and only some forty shares had as yet been taken for the proposed model Kindergarten and training school.

In June, 1844, Froebel went, by the invitation of Karl Schneider, to Sachsenhausen, near Frankfurt-am-Main; where, with Middendorff's assistance, he gave a lecture and demonstration in the infant school. They next went to Ingelheim to open a new Kindergarten, and then to Heidelberg, to see Leonhardi, who, on his marriage with Sidonie Krause, in 1839, had settled there as professor at the University. Middendorff sent Leonhardi the following poem in commemoration of this visit:—

"O Heidelberg, ich denke dein!
Du ziehst den Blick aus weiter Ferne
Dir nach, gleich einem goldnen Sterne,
Zu deinen Bergen, Hügeln, Au'n.

Wie ruhest du, O Stadt so schön!
So gross geschmückt vom alten Schlosse,
Das auf dem festen Felsenschoosse
Die Kaiser bau'ten sich zum Throu.

Wie ruhest du so wohlbewahrt!
Die Bergeshäupter sich umkrönen
Mit Zeichen vor den Heldensöhnen!
Und Buchenschatten hüllt dich ein.

Wie ruhest du so wohlgenährt!
Es tränken dich des Neckars Fluten,
Es stärken dich der Reben Gluten,
Das Leben strömt dir Fülle zu.

O Heidelberg, ich denke dein!
Den Freund ich wieder hier gefunden
Und mit der Gattin treu verbunden;
Uns ein't der schönern Menschheit Ziel.

O Stadt wie hast du mich beglückt!
Ich sah ein stilles Mutterleben
So lauter innig hingegeben
Dem hohen Ruf, dem Kinderheil.

O kleine Stadt wie gross bist du!
Du lässt den Weisen niedersteigen
Und Forscher sich den Kindlein neigen,
Zu sichern ihrer Menschheit Schritt.

O segne, Gott, die schöne Stadt!
Erfreu' den Greis in Silberhaaren,
Beschirm die frohen Kinderschaaren;
Lass sie die bessre Zukunft schau'n."

In July Froebel went to Darmstadt, where he made a most important convert in the person of Dr. Julius Foelsing,* Principal of the Cadet School at Darmstadt. In a letter to Leonardi he says: "Here, as elsewhere, dear Leonhardi, I see many a sign of your good work for the cause. Thanks to your preparation, Darmstadt is now ready for the appointment of a Kindergärtnerin."†

Foelsing's methods interested Froebel and Middendorff exceedingly. Middendorff was especially pleased with the children's musical training, and begged Foelsing to allow them to help him illustrate a lecture he was about to give on the Mothers Songs. This was arranged, and to Middendorff's great delight, Foelsing made the children sing his own song, "Here stands a little house." Foelsing did not always agree with our two educationists, and he was inclined to scoff at the new name, and at what he, with a little sly malice, called Froebel's constant "berhyming and besinging." But he was charmed with Middendorff, and would dearly like to have kept him. Ida Seele's intelligence, gentleness, and devotion, too, he regarded as priceless. By the time Froebel left Darmstadt, he not only promised to be faithful to the Froebel principles, but even to adopt the name "Kindergarten." Froebel left Darmstadt in November, and

---

* Dr. Julius Foelsing, born in 1816, was not yet thirty years of age. He was a pupil of Diesterweg; had been an educationist from the age of nineteen; had invented a system of his own, which had been tried with great success for over ten years. Diesterweg says he was the most prolific and best-known writer on infant education in Germany. With Froebel's help he now started a Frobelian infant school for the well-to-do, under Fraulein Ida Seele, a Blankenburg teacher. He was also the founder of a Pedagogic Society, which was the means of training four hundred infant mistresses.

† This is the first time we find the word in Froebel's handwriting.

went, by way of Mainz and Ingelheim, to Frankfurt, where two of his disciples were occupying themselves with some little action songs for young children. Froebel contributed many which he had worked out during his stay in Darmstadt. These are very simple, being mostly the result of actual observation of children whilst playing spontaneously. One of these games originated in the following manner:—There happened to be a slender support in the middle of the children's play-room at Blankenburg, and children always delight in turning round a pole. This column seemed to have a magnetic effect upon them; the moment they were free to do as they liked, everyone wanted to get hold of it, and there was a regular skirmish as to who could join the little crowd twirling round. Seeing this, Froebel devised a way of bringing order into the game without too much interference, and his suggestions were heartily welcomed. Four or eight children were allowed to grasp the column with one hand, whilst stretching out the other to a little companion, who, in his turn, did the same to another, making radiating lines round the column. The smallest were placed nearest the column, so as to leave the greater effort to the bigger children. They turned at first very gently, and got gradually quicker and quicker; the little mill song was added in order to regulate the movement:

"Blow, wind, blow, and go, mill, go,
   That the miller may grind his corn,
   That the baker may take it, and into rolls make it,
      And bring us some hot in the morn."

To Froebel's great delight he found the children playing this game again and again, and eagerly adopting any suggestions he was able to make, such as every now and again turning the other way, changing miller or baker. When they had to play in the open air, or in a room without a column, the teacher would stand in the middle with a thick cord round his waist for the children to slip their little fingers into, or a tree trunk might serve the same purpose. Other games were modifications of this, such as the star, the crown, the wind-mill.

On his way to Frankfurt Froebel met Dr. Schliephacke,* tutor to the Prince of Nassau. "We travelled together," he says, "and found our interest in education a great bond of union between us. He thoroughly grasped our idea. Whether this acquaintance will bring us more than social advantages I do not know. In any case, however, we have in this gentleman a true friend of children, who will co-operate with us from his own point of view. He will help us to prove that there is a great gap in education; that the proper treatment of children is little understood, and that in our system lies the secret of supplying what is wanting. We discussed the attitude of the State toward the cause, and agreed that the conversion of Darmstadt and Heidelberg would be a great step."

Froebel thought that Kindergarten songs should represent the simple language and simple ideas of children, just as national songs do those of a nation; and that wherever they are true to childhood they become classical as these are. He and his friends worked out over one hundred ball games in connection

---

* In his contribution to the report of the Philosophical Congress at Frankfurt, in 1869, Dr. Schliephacke testified warmly to the excellence of Froebel's work. He died in 1873.

with the first gift, the melodies being composed by Kohl, and the movements suggested by those natural to little children—marching, running, jumping, sliding, rolling, twirling, flying, wandering—movements, in short, indicated by such games as "The Brooklet," "Snail," and "Mill Wheel." Also a large number of games for the special exercise of the limbs and fingers were added. Froebel put these little games at the disposal of his teachers, not with the idea that they should be played everywhere and with all children just in the same way. "On the contrary," he says, "these are just samples of what may be done with the little ones; but the true Kindergärtnerin will listen to the suggestions of the children, and will be guided by circumstances in her treatment of the game.* The best Kindergarten games are the result of following the children's lead. And the best rhymes and songs for little children are those which suggest themselves to those actually working with them. The games are the central feature of the Kindergarten system. Hence, they should express the child's mind, and satisfy his instincts more fully than anything else. They are little dramas in which the child is able to express his own thought in his own way; and this expression or "Darstellung" enables him to understand his own doings and those of others, and to realise the world around him, which, without his own activity, would be but a vision or a dream. The child is always

* KOEHLER's *Action Songs*, published in 1862, were the first *collection* suitable for general use in the Kindergarten. In his introduction he shows how the children welcome the co-operation of teacher, mother, aunt, or friend in their games, and how pleased they are to be shown *how* to carry out their ideas without the disorder and confusion which often results from their own want of judgment.

ready to join in the little performance, and carry out the ideas produced in his mind by the little songs, recitations, and discussions that form part of the game. His frequent '*let me do it*' shows his consciousness of power, and his natural desire to exercise it. We should respect this instinct for self-activity, and beware of doing everything for the child. As long as the ideas dealt with are such as appeal to the child's mind, there is no need for the teacher to do anything for him. Only provide suitable objects, encourage suitable actions, and use suitable words, *i.e.*, such as he can understand, and you will find him full of zeal and energy. It is only unsuitable tasks that stultify and deaden him."

A Parents' Union was formed in December, 1844, for the purpose of making the home life of young children more regularly educational. "What we want," Froebel wrote to Leonhardi, "is the formation everywhere of associations (without class distinction) of parents and others who will endeavour to start a reform in family, social, and national life. Such associations would make it their business—(1) To enquire into existing conditions of education, whether for private and domestic, or for social and public life; (2) To find the means of education in these different directions; (3) The means being found, to see them actually utilised. The Froebel schools need not of necessity be the main point of discussion. The time for considering the Kindergarten system should follow, not precede, an enquiry into the nature of man and the needs of childhood. The subject should be made to attract general attention. One of the Baden papers might serve to bring it to the notice of citizens, farmers, and labourers.

Those whose vocations imply the study of plants and the organic world generally, might be led to extend their observations to the development of man. I look to you to rouse the Heidelbergers to take an interest in this all-important subject. It lies at the root of all we wish to bring about, and Heidelberg and Baden generally would be excellent soil for such seed." As a first result of Froebel's effort a union of parents was formed at Eichfeld (February, 1845), and Froebel sought, by a vigorous correspondence, to make it known in the educational world.

Keilhau was now in a very flourishing condition, and boasted of some promising students; and as the Blankenburg training school hardly paid its way, it was thought best to carry over the students to the mother institution, and so save the double training staff. Froebel felt, however, that if anything serious was to be done, leaders in education must be induced to take an interest in the movement. Hence he was glad to be summoned to Dresden to Adolf Frankenberg's marriage. It seems that some time in 1844 Frankenberg had made the acquaintance of Louise Hermann, niece of Professor Hermann, of Dorpat, in whom he found a ready convert to the doctrines of Krause and Froebel. The friendship of the two young people ended in their marriage on the 21st April, 1845. On the day of the wedding a procession of children brought flowers and wedding presents to the bride, who, after treating them to chocolate and cakes, joined Frankenberg and Froebel in leading the games. She was evidently quite in her element amongst the children. Indeed, her father had said of her when she was only six years old, that he was sure she had the teacher in her. Froebel spent a fortnight in Dresden, teaching his games to her and the children. The enthusiasm of "the new Tante," and her influence with her friends and acquaintances, soon raised the number of pupils from forty to eighty. Froebel's work with her for this short time, however, only served to make her realise her own shortcomings, and at Christmas (1847) she went to study at Keilhau. It was only by dint of great self-sacrifice that Frankenberg had been able to obtain the necessary authorisation for the establishment of a State Kindergarten in Dresden, and in spite of the support of such men as the Minister, Von Lindenau, and Dr. Vogel, of Leipzig, progress was but slow.

Froebel was meantime using his utmost endeavours to establish a union of teachers in Dresden. From Dresden he went to Halle to make the acquaintance of Pastor Wislicenus; thence to visit Pastor Uhlich, in Magdeburg. Carefully avoiding all share in political and religious agitations, he devoted himself to his mission of educational reform. There were as yet few genuine Froebel schools, and he could see at first but little result of his travels. "But I am fully convinced," he said, "that those who come after me, though they may know less of this matter, will have a far higher reward; the myth of the Sybilline books is true even in our day."

Further educational journeys were undertaken by Froebel during the year 1846. He passed through the valleys of the Saal, the Elster, the Malde, and the Elbe. He visited Halle, Wittenberg, Sorgau, and Glauchau, sowing everywhere the seeds of hope and inspiration, and always affirming his belief in the ultimate spread of the system. Froebel's irrepressible hopefulness and unquenchable zeal were destined to have their reward, for he lived to see many a gifted woman and future pioneer of the Froebel cause devote herself heart and soul to the mastery of the system. Some of these attended his course on the "Active Instincts of the Child," given on his return to Keilhau in the autumn.

From this time forward Froebel devoted himself chiefly to the education of women.* He felt with Schiller that the salvation of any country must depend upon its women.† Froebel's principles of evolution naturally led him to the woman as the starting-point for the child's education. It was amongst women that he found sympathy and understanding, which men as yet were unable to give him. The mother with her babe was the one who could best realise his aims and ideals. In the earlier days he had been inclined to set her a pattern of educational devices. Now that he knew her better he expected her to lead, and he was not disappointed. In 1847 a successful Kindergarten festival was organised at Quetz, near Halle. Froebel delivered an address on the principle of the Kindergarten games and occupations. Earnestness and unanimity of purpose characterised this meeting, and all were charmed with Froebel's exposition of the subject.

The training course given at Keilhau in the winter of 1847 was attended by Alwina Middendorff, Frau Frankenberg, and Luise Levin, who had for two years

---

* With a view to a more perfect family life, Froebel proposed that girls should have this training as a preparation for marriage.

† "Nature intended woman for her masterpiece."—LESSING.

filled the post of house-mother at Keilhau. These three ladies, as well as Emma Habich and Fräulein Stieler, did much to spread the system. Fräulein Levin writes: "Keilhau opened up a new world to me. When not in Froebel's class, I used to take my work and sit in his room. I looked upon him as one of the greatest benefactors of mankind, and my only longing was to show my gratitude by faithful work."* Another of the Keilhau pupils was Augusta Traberth, a very gifted Kindergärtnerin, who lately celebrated the twenty-fifth anniversary of her work at Eisenach; but the most distinguished of the Keilhau students at this time was Henrietta Breymann, who founded an excellent institution at Watzum. She lectured with great success at Brussels, and was appointed to assist in the reorganisation of the Belgian schools.† The success of these ladies was partly due to their innate genius, but also in a great measure to Froebel's wonderful power of rousing the intelligence and enthusiasm of women. It was, perhaps, through the woman's influence that the artistic treatment of the gifts and occupations was made so prominent.‡ The young girls easily mastered the occupations, and soon learned to use them as a means of training the children's intelligence and skill.

Froebel had learned in his educational tours the value of demonstration and explanation, and he now

* Luise Levin had her wish, for in 1851 she became Froebel's second wife.

† This lady married Dr. Schrader, a railway director, and became the Principal of the Pestalozzi Institute at Berlin. On p. 332 of *Hanschmann*, probably through a misprint, she is confounded with Fräulein Ida Seele.

‡ Froebel's own tendency was rather to treat them from a mathematical point of view.

proposed to call a Conference of German teachers and educators, to discuss and test the Kindergarten system as an integral part of national education. In June, 1848, a circular was sent out to teachers and friends of education. A few quotations will show the drift of it:—

"All Germany is looking for a reform in education; this must be brought about by a perfecting of our national system, not merely of elementary, secondary, advanced or higher schools, but of the whole educational system, and more especially of that part which precedes the school proper. If the building is to be solid, we must look to the foundations. The home education of rich and poor alike must be improved and supplemented. Parents often lack the time, means, and skill necessary for the development of their children's powers. And even if they knew how to train them on any system in harmony with nature, they are too little acquainted with the schools to which they send them to prepare them adequately for their work. It therefore behoves the State to establish institutions for the education of children, of parents, and of those who are to become parents. If through ignorance and indifference little children are treated improperly, it is the business of all who love their nation to alter this state of things."

In June, 1848, a circular was issued inviting "teachers and lovers of children to an educational Congress at Keilhau, near Rudolstadt," where Friedrich Froebel had been at work for the "past thirty years." This circular was signed by Froebel and a number of teachers and professors. It was finally decided to hold the meeting in the town of Rudolstadt itself; and the following invitation appeared in the *Citizen:*—"The Rudolstädters hope to have the pleasure of receiving the teachers and others attending the Conference, and they trust that the modest hospitality they are able to offer will be accepted." Special invitations, signed by Froebel and the other members of the Conference Committee, were sent to some of the more distinguished friends of the cause.

Many came to the meeting armed with ready-made objections to the system; some being founded on ignorance, some on a conservative feeling which made them fear any innovation. Many, of course, were unable to see the need of any organised system for children under the school age, and far less able to compare the needs of these little ones with those of the school child. It was argued that the daily habit of play would produce loiterers and triflers, and altogether unfit the children for school work.*

One of the fiercest opponents to the system was Julius Kell, of Leipzig. Indeed, some of the questions he put to Froebel were so "inquisitorial," says an eye-witness, that even Kell's own allies protested, and stood up in Froebel's defence. Froebel's answers to all objections were very patient and clear-headed; and he and his colleagues so ably defended the system that the Congress ended by a unanimous acknowledgment of its soundness and truth.

Pastor Habig, in summing up the various speeches, concluded with the following appeal to the assembly: "We have probably," he said, "not yet reached perfection in the application of this system. There may be details to which it would be wise for us to apply our best judgment and experience, but surely the

---

* This objection was most ably answered by August Koehler, in the introduction to his collection of games and songs, which is well worth reading.

teachers and educators present cannot withhold their sympathy and approval from so excellent a system of training the young." But in spite of the favourable resolution passed by the Conference, the Froebel teachers felt that the objections to the system which had been expressed by several present demanded more serious attention than it had been possible to give them at the time. Hence Middendorff sent to the German Parliament, in 1848, a carefully-written essay in defence of the Kindergarten as a necessary part of modern education. Dr. Wichard Lange wrote a preface to the second edition (1861), in which he says: "The Kindergarten system has as yet had no fair trial, but in this little book Middendorff gives very clearly its *raison d'être*, and its methods and practices."

In the winter of 1848 Froebel was invited to give a training course in Dresden, where Luise Frankenberg had worked up a class of students. His power of work was enormous. He gave three lectures daily; one in the morning to some foreign students who lived with Frankenberg, another in the afternoon, and a third in the evening. These classes were a brilliant success, and made Dresden an important centre for the system. Amongst the more distinguished students who came under Froebel's influence this winter was the gifted and amiable Marquart, who, like Froebel, had begun his educational career by teaching some young relatives. He and his wife and daughters became enthusiastic Froebelians, and sent out many a first-rate Kindergarten teacher. "It shall not be said," wrote Bruno Marquart, "that Friedrich Froebel worked in vain in Dresden; if no one else will found a Kindergarten I will do it myself." And this he did (in spite of a good deal of opposition). In Marquart's school the Kindergarten and the lower forms of the school proper formed a continuous and well-graded whole.

Amongst the Dresden pupils was Frl. Dahlenkamp, niece of Gustav Kühne, who established a Kindergarten at Leipzig. Dr. Herz, too, attended with his gifted wife, who did so much for children of weak intellect. Her writings were the means of introducing the system into several institutions, and she herself applied it in her husband's asylum at Meissen. Other names mentioned in this connection are Amelia Marschner, Bertha Gloeckner, and Herr Ritz, who, with Adolf Frankenberg, was amongst the first advocates for gymnastics for women; Frankenberg himself, with his wife and his assistant, Frl. Busch, attended the Dresden course.*

A good deal had been done by the end of the year 1849 for the elaboration of the gifts and occupations. Sticks and tablets were added as a means for proceeding from solids to planes and lines.† Also an intermediate form (the cylinder) had been added to

---

* After Frankenberg's death, in 1858, his wife went to Jena, and devoted her originality and skill to Dr. Keferstein's institution. She did not consider herself, when over fifty years of age, too old to play Kindergarten games with the children. She had seen Froebel conduct many a game when he was seventy. Kohl, too, the composer of the *Kose-Lieder*, was in Froebel's class in Dresden, and undertook to drill the ladies in the singing of his little songs. "It is no wonder," said Luise Frankenberg, "that we thoroughly understood how to sing them." He used to make us hum them very gently, almost like speaking; as if they had just been improvised."

† Perforation was introduced as a further geometrical abstraction, dealing with points only; but it is a somewhat dangerous occupation on account of the nature of the tool used.

the second gift. All the exercises were based on the discovery of contrasts or conciliation of contrasts. This principle was probably derived by Froebel from what Schelling calls "Laws of Polarity," and Hegel "Dialectic Development."

As an explanation of the name Kindergarten the word "garden" has been traced philologically to limit, circle, uniting, boundary. Froebel's garden is a place in which the children are surrounded by such conditions as allow them freedom of growth for body, mind, and spirit, and in which their powers develop in harmony and beauty. The name "garden" thus indicates the treatment Froebel desires for the children. They are to be like plants under the care of a "skilful gardener."

CHAPTER X.

FROEBEL THE APOSTLE OF WOMEN.

1849 TO 1851. MARIENTHAL.

Liebenstein—Diesterweg and Froebel—The Hamburg Women's Union—Karl Froebel—Women Pioneers—Middendorff and Froebel in Hamburg—The School for Mothers—Higher Education for Girls—Froebel's Main Principles—Festival at Altenstein—Froebel's Second Marriage—Frau Luise Froebel—The Life at Marienthal—Personal Recollections of Froebel—Hostility of the Prussian Government.

HOPING once more to interest the Duke of Meiningen in his work, Froebel went in the spring of 1849 to Bad-Liebenstein. He and his friends had decided that Marienthal, near Liebenstein, would be a perfect spot for a training school for women. Liebenstein is a health resort, much frequented by Germans on account of its salubrious springs and the beauty of its situation. The country is undulating and rich in vegetation. The air is sweet and fresh, and filled with the scent of the pine woods and the song of birds.

Amongst the visitors at Bad-Liebenstein in the summer of 1848 was Adolph Diesterweg,* the editor of the *Wegweiser*, whose wife was staying there for her health. On the day of his arrival, some time in July, sitting under the trees in front of the Kurhaus, he asked what there was to see at Liebenstein, whereupon

---

* Foelsing's trainer and teacher.

one of the guests told him there was one sight he must on no account miss, "an old fool who plays about with the village children." Nothing more was said at the time, but the next day his friend, Frau von Marenholtz, invited him to go with her to see a school under the direction of Herr Froebel. He had heard of Froebel as an eccentric man, whose notion was that children should learn everything in play; and putting two and two together, he surmised that Froebel must be the "old fool" his friends had alluded to the day before.

The following somewhat disdainful words had appeared in an early number of the *Wegweiser*:—*
"I ought, perhaps, to mention Froebel, of Rudolstadt, in this connection (infant education), but as I have had no opportunity of seeing his work I can form no judgment. The somewhat exaggerated accounts I have met with are rather calculated to make one mistrust the system."

It is evident that Diesterweg knew Froebel only from hearsay, or from unsatisfactory explanations of his object. He only understood him after making his personal acquaintance. One visit to Marienthal, however, sufficed to convince him that he was in the presence of a great educator; and, in his dedication of the fourth number of his journal to the wonderful man ("this magician amongst the maidens and little children"), there is something like a tone of regret that he had not known him sooner. Frau von Marenholtz had had some difficulty in persuading him to accompany her to the farm-house where Froebel was at work with his forty peasant children. But once there, he came

---

* Only three numbers were out at the time.

under the spell of the old man's gentleness and tact. He repeated his visit, and saw Froebel conduct some games in the open air; a large circle was formed, and eight or ten young girls took their places in it. The children, whose ages varied from two to eight or ten years, were evidently very poor. Some were barefooted, some bareheaded, and some in rags.

They were playing with the utmost vigour and delight, however, and Froebel was a very child amongst them. Many of the games are now familiar to us, *e.g.*, the Fishes, the Pigeons, the Cuckoo. When the games were over the children were led off in procession singing their closing song. After this, Diesterweg accompanied Frau von Marenholtz in her daily visits to Froebel. He would knock at her door with the *Mutter-und Kose-Lieder* under his arm, and say, "Are you ready to go to school?"* They joined the Froebel students in their lessons and in their rambles over the hills with the master, and it was not long before a hearty friendship was formed between the two great Pestalozzian teachers. Diesterweg, who certainly was one of the most distinguished pedagogues of his time, once convinced, gave himself heart and soul to Froebel and his cause, and henceforth did all he could to advance the movement. He counted the hours spent with Froebel amongst his most treasured recollections.

* The visitors at Liebenstein seem to have had some fun over these big school children. They were called "Eisel und Beisel," and some witty guest, on meeting them on one of their rambles with Froebel, in earnest conversation, exclaimed, "There go the way, the truth, and the life."—*Reminiscences of Froebel*, ch. i.

"Mere words can give no idea," says Diesterweg, "of the natural grace and happiness of the Kindergarten children, nor of the devotion with which Froebel works at his cause. Year by year, day by day, hour by hour he is occupied with it. Come who will, and when he will, nothing can check his ardour. I have seen nothing like it in all my life. His mind is entirely possessed by his idea."

Froebel met Diesterweg again in the autumn, when he went to Hamburg at the instigation of his old pupils, Alwina Middendorff and Doris Lütkens.*

These enthusiastic Froebelians rather hoped the Hamburg Women's Union would take up Froebel's work, especially as two of its delegates had visited Froebel at Liebenstein, and had been much impressed by what they saw. But the Union aimed rather at the social and political advancement of women than at their culture in Froebel's sense; and had already started a correspondence with Professor Karl Froebel, Froebel's nephew, in Zurich, with reference to the establishment of an advanced girls' school in Hamburg.†

Middendorff accompanied his friend to Hamburg. He was glad of the opportunity of seeing his daughter, who was her father's pupil, and a true educationist.

* Doris Lütkens had been persuaded by her friend Alwina to go to Rudolstadt and study with Froebel. It was she who drew the attention of the Hamburg Women's Union to Froebel's work.

† This school was intended to give girls the opportunity of studies such as their brothers enjoyed at the university; to be, in short, a kind of Girton or Newnham. Certain members of the Union, especially the delegates Frau Wüstenfeld and Bertha Traun, were warm advocates of the girls' high school, and the matter ended by an invitation being sent to the younger Froebel to come to Hamburg and start the girls' school.

She had started several Kindergartens, and had converted many to the cause, not the least important of her converts being her *fiancée*, Dr. Wichard Lange. Lange studied the subject carefully, and his writings have done much to make the system known. Middendorff, immediately on his arrival in Hamburg, invited friends and opponents of the system to a discussion, and opened the meeting with an address, which was so convincing that it almost disarmed opposition.

Dr. Wichard Lange was amongst the audience, and says: "His simple manner, white locks, and beaming countenance, charmed everyone. He began his speech gently, almost tenderly, with closed eyes, as if in reverence of his subject. But as he proceeded his voice grew louder and louder, and his eloquence and animation increased. Then, as his countenance seemed to express, a pitying regret that he could find no words to convey the depth of his conviction."

Froebel gave an address at Frl. Lütkens', in which he described the kind of instruction he wished to give to the women students in Hamburg. He also delivered a course of lectures in the hall of the new girls' school. He explained clearly and emphatically that his desire for woman was not to make her learned, nor to provide her with increased social advantages, but to win for her the development of her best and noblest qualities. Only so would the world be made happier, and would man himself be enabled with dignity to fulfil his duties to his fellow-man, to God, and to nature. Froebel's object was different from Fichte's, and even from that of his master, Pestalozzi. His aim was to rouse to the utmost, and win over to the service of early education the whole strength of womanhood.

Young girls were to be inspired to care for early childhood. This would ennoble family relations and family life, and add vastly to the sum of human happiness.

"Women," says Schleiermacher, "are destined to develop the first germs in the child's mind in all their simplicity and purity, before they have been exposed to any perverting influence; and those who take upon themselves this solemn duty should guard the sacred fire like vestal virgins." And Ziegenbein says: "It is to mothers we must look for the safe-guarding of moral and social purity; it is they who have most power to secure to their daughters a feeling for virtue and piety. It is they who hand over to the world the unacknowledged gift of leader, hero, law-giver, discoverer, artist, scientist, orator, or poet. It is, in short, the mother who exerts upon humanity the strongest influence for good or evil. Thus women render a more important service to society and the State than do men." F. Bernhardt says: "There is no better foundation for the well-being of a nation than the heart of a true mother. In the hands of parents lie heaven and hell." Froebel says: "All agree that, compared with the true mother, the formal educator is but a bungler. But she must become conscious of her own aim, and must learn intelligently to use the means to reach it. She can no longer afford to squander or neglect the earliest years of her child. As the world grows older we become richer in knowledge and in art. But childhood (the receptive period) remains short as before; and we must learn to adapt ourselves to constantly varying conditions, and to understand that what suited a previous age is no longer fitting for our own. The task of modern times is to introduce order and proportion into life, and the initiative lies with *mothers*."

The latest development of the Froebel idea was fully expressed in a periodical republished at Liebenstein in January, 1850, under the editorship of Dr. Wichard Lange, and called the *Wochenschrift*. This paper was an important contribution to modern pedagogy. It treated the Kindergarten system from a philosophical and a psychological point of view, and contained some excellent articles on early education, notes of songs and games, and a story after the manner of Pestalozzi's "How Lena learns to read." In one of his articles Froebel demands that the "noble destiny of one half the human race be acknowledged by the other, and that the sex as a whole take up its true moral and intellectual position." "Woman," he says, "will win this position for herself when she becomes conscious of her true mission. Fit or not fit, she must of necessity be the first educator of the child. It is she who strikes the keynote for his future and gives the bent to his life. After-life can only develop the germs she has implanted. Woman's love and child love are one, and we shall never do justice to either until we learn to recognise the indissoluble bond that unites them. God has planted in the mother's heart the very existence of the race. If a complicated civilization has come between mother and child, it is for us to reunite them.* Train the mother, and you train the child. Make the mother conscious of a goal

---

* Froebel's object was to unite and join what man and his conventions had so often parted,—boy and girl, old and young, rich and poor, learned and simple.

to be reached, and give her the means to reach it, and you set childhood free from all the evils of convention and routine. A mother will soon outstrip the pedagogue in her understanding of the methods to be employed for the good of her child.* But neither Pestalozzi's nor any other book can suffice for the training of the mother. The poorer mothers have neither the time nor the capacity to master the lessons in books. If all mothers are to share in the education of the young generation, there must be national Kindergartens, which, in the first instance, may serve as training schools for mothers."

What Froebel longed to see in Germany was a system of national Kindergartens which would receive the children of the poor, and train the maidens of the rich at the same time. He thought that the culture required for the proper treatment of children would be more profitable to young girls than much of the customary book learning. And he also thought that if this kind of culture were once introduced, it would ultimately have its effect on the girls' school education, and tend to make it more practical and less artificial. Conventional school education offers, according to Froebel, too little scope for the girl's sense of art and poetry, and makes too great a separation between her and her natural duties and sympathies. It is natural, he says, for a young girl to love little children.

> "Wo wie ein unergründlich Meer
> Ein Kinderauge blaut,
> Du hast dem Herrn, O, schaue her,
> Ins Auge selbst geschaut.

---

* Though Froebel's teaching is pre-eminently the teaching for mothers, he recommends again and again the training of both sexes as Kindergarten teachers.

> Ein Kindesblick, ein Blick des Herrn,
> Vor dem das Herz erschrickt;
> Ein Blick des Herrn, ein Friedenstern,
> Der Trost und Ruhe blickt.
>
> Und warst Du je so rein und fromm;
> Ach, warst Du je ein Kind?
> Verzage nicht, komm wieder komm!
> Und sei wie Kinder sind."

Karl Froebel shared his uncle's views on the importance of woman's influence as first educator, and in his school at Hamburg he not only provided the girls with opportunity for academic study, but also made an attempt to train them for motherhood and for social duties. The graces of life were promoted by such subjects as literature, foreign languages, mythology, and art. Froebel held with Wiese that "woman's education should take its tone from the family and the home."* But he acknowledged that neither the home nor the school offer a complete education; learning and love are both necessary. He recommended the grouping of families into small educational associations, so that the education of their children might be placed under the direction of philosophers and educationists. In short, an enlarged family with enlarged means of obtaining the best conditions for the children."†

Karl Froebel's scheme of education included a Kindergarten department, a day school, boarding schools for boys and girls, a normal school for men teachers, and an advanced school for women, who were to be trained in family and social duties, and to learn art and

---

* All women have a motherly mission, even though they be not mothers, and usefulness in family and social life is their best profession.

† See KARL SCHMIDT's *History of Pedagogy.*

science with a view to the beautifying and ennobling of life. Science for them was not to be treated as an abstract subject, but studied only as far as it is applicable to human life. Karl Froebel maintained that every woman should be so educated as to win for herself an independent economic position.

His special education for girls began somewhere about the thirteenth year, at the period when difference of sex makes itself felt. The boys at this age were put through a strictly scientific course of mathematics, language, and logic, to which, however, were added nature studies and art as far as it was applicable to these; also a certain amount of musical culture. The curriculum for the girls included the elements of mathematics, astronomy, and perspective; physiology, hygiene, and nursing; history, literature, and enough philosophy to understand the development of the reasoning powers.

Unfortunately for Froebel his ideas and his objects were confused with his nephew's in the minds of the public, and this led to great trouble for Froebel later on. Froebel left his mark in Hamburg, however, where, before leaving, he founded two Kindergartens, each with upwards of sixty children. On his return to Liebenstein, in the spring of 1850, he took up his abode in a shooting lodge at Marienthal which his friend the Baroness of Marenholtz-Bulow had induced the Duke of Meiningen to put at his disposal.

A few personal recollections will best give an idea of his work there. "I would have missed anything," wrote one student, "rather than the happy time at Marienthal, and I regret every minute not passed with Froebel. I remember how, on one occasion, as we stood watching the sunset, the dear master had kind words for us all. At another time how he drew our attention to the beautiful colours in the dewdrops; then how delighted he was with the decoration of the rooms on his return from Gotha: what a sweet remembrance it is!"

And this testimony to the affection and enthusiasm he inspired is confirmed by the letters received from many a grateful pupil on his birthday in 1851. "I only wish that every human being," wrote one, "could have the benefit of your education. I know how much happiness it gives." And another, "I wish everyone knew you and your teaching. I congratulate myself on having learned to work with little children. It has taught me to reflect before acting, and to order my thoughts and my life. Life has become more sacred to me, and I hope that these experiences will be a support in whatever dark days there may be in store for me."

There was a constant stream of visitors to the institution at Marienthal, and as Froebel became more and more popular, he formed the subject of much interest and discussion in the neighbourhood. Some looked upon him as "the prophet of a new development for humanity," "the lawgiver of a new education," "the apostle of woman's freedom"; whilst others described him as "a fool," "a fanatic," or "an impostor."

"One evening in the week was reserved at Marienthal for demonstrations and discussions, and visitors were invited to join both. The guests generally found Froebel playing with a crowd of peasant children and young teachers of both sexes."

"It was touching to see the children's affection for

Froebel. They would run towards the tall figure the moment it came into sight, and would hang about him and climb on his knee, and when he spoke, even the most turbulent would listen impressed and reverent.

"One day, in the midst of the singing, a little five-year-old boy, who had been brought into the ring by his mother, began to cry, said he would not play, and insisted also that his mother should come out of the ring. The mother remained, however, and the child continued to disturb the game; Froebel took the little one upon his knee, and showed him the cube spinning on a thread, whereupon he began to smile, and was soon seen joining the ring with Froebel. He never troubled them any more. When the games were over, the little ones would clamour round him and entreat him to play with them again and again. Lines of thought were visible on his high forehead; but as he bent over the children, the long white hair falling over his eyes, his face would beam with affection, and he would take a little hand in his, or pat a little curly pate in a kindly, encouraging way. They called him 'Father,' and in his response he would put a world of tenderness into the words, 'My child.' When all was over the children would file off in pairs, singing a parting song as they went."*

"Singing is the best accompaniment to everything for children," he said, in his hearty, convincing way. "It was by singing that the Greeks learned their *Homer*, and it is thus we can best learn our mother-

---

* Surely this makes as beautiful a picture of "child-love" as one could imagine, and reminds one of Pestalozzi amongst his children at Stanz.

tongue."* This was not mere sentimentality with Froebel,† but may rather be attributed to a certain poetic simplicity with which he did everything. "He was full of enthusiasm and belief in his mission, and gave one the idea of being a priest of nature," says Kuehne; "and this it was that so much impressed and influenced women."

After the departure of the children the guests at Keilhau would proceed to the large hall of the house, where the long table was covered with gifts and occupations, not in the form of a grand exhibition, but just simple specimens of the work done by Kindergarten children. Froebel would dwell upon the industry, the perseverance, and the ingenuity required to produce these specimens. Sometimes a visitor would try his hand at one or other of the occupations, or the whole company would set to work upon the gifts and materials before them, Froebel himself being one of the first to be carried away by the fascination of inventing combinations and designs. Indeed, he was often so intent upon his work that he forgot there were any visitors present."

Froebel regarded his work at Marienthal as the culminating point of his educational effort. It expressed his highest conception of education. Women were to him the "harmonisers of human life." Frau von Marenholtz succeeded in interesting the Duchess of Meiningen in the work, and a festival was organised at Altenstein to mark the birth of the Marienthal institution. This celebration took place on August 4,

---

* "In the childhood of the world common speech was song."—JEAN PAUL RICHTER.

† It was not the mere berhyming and besinging Foelsing suggested.

1850, the meeting-place being the park surrounding the Castle of Altenstein. Here, on a grassy plateau, about three hundred children from the neighbouring villages and towns assembled, and went through their exercises and evolutions. They marched in order until eight concentric rings were formed, whereupon all joined in the opening song:

> "Seht uns hier in Vereine,
> Dass die Eintracht erscheine
> In dem heiteren Spiel;
> Ordnung schön uns verbinde,
> Liebe in allem sich finde,
> Bringe der lieblichen Früchte so viel."

The circles then changed into a long, undulating line, and the children sang "Like a little ball of twine," as they marched along, winding in and out amongst the trees, twisting themselves into a close spiral or ball, and untwisting again. Then they formed different circles, so that each Kindergarten might play the games specially prepared for the occasion.* After the Marienthal children had played some Kindergarten games, the Salzungen children were placed in two groups, the boys doing some gymnastics, whilst the girls played at "La Grace." Then again all formed rings for "Cat and Mouse," played to music. After this the whole company marched in procession towards the castle for rest and refreshment. Games then followed which were more or less familiar to all, such as "Little children when they're good," "Hand in hand here we stand," "In a row marching so,"

* What an excellent plan it would be for Kindergartens to co-operate in this way to make the system known to the public. How much they would teach and how much they would learn by co-operation.

"With game and song we march along," "The Oak-wreath," "Roses and Lilies," "The Dove-cote," "The Snail." At sunset the happy meeting dispersed; and the effect was imposing and touching as the long procession moved in its rhythmic way to the tune of the parting song, their voices growing fainter and fainter, gradually disappearing in the distance. Froebel received many an assurance of the success of this festival.

"I am thankful," said one, "that my business led me hither to-day. I could not help weeping tears of regret as I looked at the happy groups, and thought of my own children at home missing it all. How often have I wished them here to-day."

"The gentleness and affection with which the children are treated by your teachers is a touching sight," said another.

"I am no Meininger, I am a Hessian, and come from Cassel," said a third; "but I should like to shake hands with you and express my gratitude. I only wish our teachers would introduce this, for it shows what children may be made to do if they are treated with kindness. Surely the blessing of heaven rests upon such a day."

"The festival at Altenstein," says Benfey, "has shown us what the child is capable of when provided with cheerful and bright surroundings, and when his instinct for development is respected. On this happy occasion there was a marvellous manifestation both of individuality and independence in the separate children and groups of children, and of unity and harmony of action amongst the whole company. Froebel's ideas evidently dominated the whole performance. Every detail was a proof of his intelligence, care, and forethought."

No history of Froebel would be complete without an account of this Altenstein festival. It was only the parent of many similar co-operative demonstrations, but it marks a new departure in the development of the Froebel system.

It was difficult for Froebel to demonstrate practically his view of "harmony of life" at Marienthal, as, for the first time for many years, he had no family life. Indeed, he realised acutely the need of a home, and of some faithful companion in whose hands he might safely leave his work when he should no longer be able to continue it. Such a friend and companion Froebel found in Luise Levin.* She was now about thirty years of age, was inspired by Froebel and his idea, and had been the Principal of his Liebenstein Training School for two years. She was a great friend of his brother Christian's family. Indeed, she had come on a visit to the Christian Froebels about five years before, and the life and spirit of Keilhau had so charmed her that she was easily persuaded to remain and help Frau Froebel in her household duties. In 1847, however, she had joined the circle of Kindergarten students then working under Froebel, and henceforth became his devoted admirer and friend, and finally the comforter of his declining years.

The Keilhau circle were not unanimous in approving of Froebel's marriage with this lady; but Middendorff, who had his friend's real interest at heart, and who believed that this marriage might bring a larger

* I believe some reminiscences of her married life were contributed by Frau Froebel to *Child Life* some time in 1889. See Appendix II. A.

number of educated women into the field, gave his hearty approval, and the ceremony took place in July, 1851. The marriage was in every way a great success, for Frau Froebel filled her somewhat difficult position with dignity, and to the satisfaction of all concerned, even of those who at first were inclined to disapprove; and Froebel was comforted and soothed by the thought of leaving his name and work in such good hands. She was a splendid house-mother, and knew how to endear herself to the students. Many letters show the delightful relationship existing between her and her pupils.

Froebel's personality always impressed his pupils in the most astonishing way; he knew how to move their innermost hearts, to cure them of all artificiality and self-consciousness, and to bring them back to simplicity and youth. His work amongst women is unique. Though childless, he has understood childhood as few parents do. "There are plenty," he would say, "who provide a physical existence for their children. Let us become spiritual parents. My children," he said, "are my ideas," and turning to his wife, he added, "I look to you to cherish them."

The happiest days of Froebel's life were now spent at Marienthal; his marriage had brought him a peace and restfulness he had never known before. But, alas! this was not to last. For whilst an unusual number of talented young women were quietly enjoying their training with Froebel in his beautiful country home, a blow fell upon him from the outer world from which he was not to recover. Before dealing with this sad episode in Froebel's history, it may be well to describe shortly the life of the master and his pupils at Marienthal, whilst still undisturbed by it. The Duke's stately shooting lodge was surrounded by park and wood. In the early summer mornings of the year 1851 a group of bright young girls might be found seated at a table under the shadow of the trees, listening with reverence to the inspired words of the old man as he marched backwards and forwards with energetic speech and sparkling eye. "I had heard of Froebel through a relative," says one of the pupils who attended this course. "At first I was somewhat repelled by his peculiar appearance, but I soon got over this, and now I can never thank him enough for the happy hours which I have spent in his company. Amongst the students was a young widow with a baby nine months old, who were Froebel's delight. On their arrival they were welcomed by a procession with wreaths and flowers, and a poem from Middendorff."*

From another student we have the following description of a day at Marienthal:—"We assembled at eight o'clock. After breakfast Froebel gave us a short address, taking as text a verse or poem which had struck him, often one of Leopold Schaefer's. At nine o'clock we had a lesson in Physiology, especially the physiology of the senses. This would lead to the subject before us.† He often made long digressions, which were somewhat difficult for us beginners to follow, but he never lost the thread of his discourse. We took notes, but we did not reproduce the lectures. Being strenuously opposed to the use of foreign words, and anxious to prove to us the riches of our own

---

* For a list of the students who took Froebel's last course at Marienthal see *Hanschmann*, pp. 414, 415.
† Probably the Kindergarten Gifts.

language, he would frequently give an object several names. At eleven o'clock we had a singing lesson from Stangenberger, who had come to Marienthal to study under Froebel. He was organist at Meiningen, and composed many Kindergarten songs.* We spent the afternoons drawing in chequers with Frau Froebel; and our leisure time was spent on occupations such as building, paper-folding, twisting, plaiting, and weaving, which we worked out under Froebel's direction. We saw little of the master except during our lessons and at meal times, or perhaps on occasions when we were able to persuade him to walk with us. At such times he was as happy and merry as a child, and he was indefatigable in his search for beetles, stones, and plants, for our instruction. Nothing escaped his notice. On the Altenstein or other neighbouring heights he would discourse to us on the beauty of the scene; and whilst the ladies prepared refreshments, Froebel would philosophise or poetise, as the spirit moved him."

"His theme," says Rudolf Benfey (another eye-witness), "was generally the unity in nature, or maybe all-sided development. He would take in with his rapid glance the whole of a landscape as he sat there, a crowd of friends around him and the young ones at his feet, following his inspired words with the utmost reverence. 'What strength and support there is in the conception of nature as one grand whole!' he would say. 'Unity in nature is the very pivot of creation. Look at the scene before us—the rocks with their pine-clad slopes, and, down below, the green meadows, the little villages, the winding streams, and

---

* Most of these may be found in AUG. KOEHLER's *Bewegungspiele*.

the deep blue river. All stand there separately, individually, and are only made into one picture for us by means of a delicate membrane in the eye, and a certain amount of knowledge and reflection. A little child would have no power of collecting trees, flowers, fields, houses, etc., into one picture. For him they still remain separate detached objects. A labourer at work no doubt sees the hills, the rivers, the fields, and the villages, but the landscape as a whole escapes him.' Froebel's thoughts and reflections would pour forth in a mighty stream, and we often had to make out the connection for ourselves. 'All education,' he said, 'must be based upon, and must tend towards, unity of life. This has been overlooked in the past. The child's mind has too often been regarded as a box into which we may throw all kinds of disconnected matter, quite unassociated with his activity: here a little bit of history, there a language or a bit of arithmetic. That is all wrong. The child is a wonderful creature; he persistently refuses the indigestible and the superfluous. That which does not unite itself with his life, and grow with his growth, is but a burden to him. The child wants to know, but he wants still more to live, to be busy, to do. And he is quite right, for whilst learning makes him conscious of things, doing makes him conscious of himself; therefore let him work.' He often compared a child's mind to a plant, reminding us that leaf, bud, stem, root, all require suitable nutriment.

"'That which earth, air, and water are to the plant, stimulus and opportunity are to the mind. Just as the plant makes its own selection, in the same way the child knows best what it can assimilate. It is for the teacher to *offer* him nutriment, but patiently to *wait* for him to take it himself.' Froebel had great respect for the child's individuality, and a horror of reckless interference with it. 'Let him develop freely,' he would say, 'and in accordance with his nature. There is a vast difference in people; let each be complete in himself, and live up to his highest.' And he was equally strong in his advocacy of an all-round development. Not that he expected the child to attain mastery on every side, but rather that no side of him should be neglected. He demanded freedom and scope for the child's powers, and the utmost encouragement for his happy instinct for *self-development.* 'Let the child live and thrive as plants do. Let him put forth his shoots and buds, and have scope for his inner impulse. Life will soon show him where his strength lies. Only let him have a chance. The child's impulse is the educator's best guide. It is because the child wants to be educated that we find it *possible* to educate him. A bright, cheerful, and stimulating atmosphere is what he wants, and is indeed the main condition for his education.'"

Froebel's appearance is thus described by one of his pupils:—"A tall, stooping figure with blue-grey eyes and a long nose, and long hair parted in the middle and stroked behind his ears. When teaching he would, if not marching up and down, sit in a basket chair, resting his hands upon the arms, and speaking with closed eyes, and he had a habit of stroking his hair first on one side, then on the other. He was at times hasty with the students, and impatient

---

* Pestalozzi says that every human being born into the world has a right to the development of his powers and faculties.

when not understood. Nothing would make him more angry than to see one of his games played in a tame and meaningless way. Julie Traberth, of Eisenach, once incurred the weight of his great displeasure by simplifying, as she thought, the game of the Spring-time. But here, as always, Middendorff was the conciliating spirit; his presence was a comfort to us, for we knew we could rely upon him for words of affection, encouragement, and appreciation. We were more intimate with him than with Froebel, who was often too overstrained to have much to say to us, for he worked incessantly. There was, however, one way of approaching him, and that was to offer him flowers, of which he was passionately fond. He could not bear to destroy even a weed. It was at the opening of the Liebenstein Kindergarten that I first saw him with children, and I shall never forget it. His serious countenance relaxed into the brightest smiles as he approached one of the smallest of the children, who seemed to recognise the child's benefactor in him. Young children soon know their friends. We were touched almost to tears as we watched the tall, stooping figure moving about in the midst of the children, gently guiding and encouraging them in their games. I was there at a most fortunate moment. Frau von Marenholtz and Diesterweg were spending the summer at Liebenstein, and we made a memorable excursion to Friedrichsroda and the Inselberg. Bormann, too, Principal of the Normal School in Berlin, joined us, and after he had seen the games and listened to Diesterweg's fascinating explanations, he made a speech full of eulogy and encouragement, which greatly delighted Froebel. Bormann, on his return to Berlin, wrote a report of his visit to Froebel, which might have quieted the fears of the Prussian Government. "One thing," he says, "struck me as being both interesting and important. In the building lesson the children were taught to develop each form from the preceding one without destroying it, so that they learned care and patience, and a respect for the existing state of things. Surely this is a good moral lesson for children, rather to build up the new from the old in an orderly way, than to hope for new things out of the ruins of the old." And further on he says, "Froebel's idea is, impress such lessons on the mind of the young child at a time when he is most sensitive. This is our best chance if we want to remodel human nature; training at this age forestalls and prevents the necessity for severity later." This friendly and appreciative attitude towards him and his work by so great an authority, little prepared him for the shock so soon to follow Bormann's return to Berlin, *i.e.*, the prohibition throughout Prussia of all Kindergarten and Froebel schools.

This fatal decree brings us to the last epoch of Froebel's life. "Those were bitter days for us all," says our authority, "when we saw our revered friend so misjudged and oppressed. But his energy never forsook him, and he continued, by writing and speech, to defend his idea to the last."

CHAPTER XI.

LAST DAYS.

1851 TO 1852. LIEBENSTEIN, GOTHA.

A Fatal Blow—Last Effort—Liebenstein Conference—Froebel's Last Birthday—Visit to the Salzung Kindergarten—Last Excursion on the Altenstein—Conference at Gotha—Illness—Death—Froebel's Characteristics—Pestalozzi and Froebel—Harmony of Life.

IT was a sad misfortune that came upon Froebel in his old age. That the practice of his system should be prohibited in a country which certainly, at that time, took the lead in educational matters, caused him acute pain and probably shortened his life.

It is hardly credible that Von Raumer, the Prussian Minister of Education, should not have been able to discriminate between Karl Froebel's views on social and political emancipation and Friedrich Froebel's free natural development; but so it was, as the following extract from his report to the Prussian Government will show:—" High schools for girls and Kindergartens, as explained by Karl Froebel, form part of the Froebel social system, which tends to bring up children atheistically. Hence schools founded on this and similar principles must be forbidden." And the following was added: " The principles of Friedrich Froebel's system, though they are expressed with more reserve than his nephew's, are no less dangerous; both agree in banishing Christianity from the education of children, so that the prohibition must include both kinds of schools."

The prohibition of Kindergartens was issued on August 7th, 1851, and came like a bomb into the peaceful circle at Marienthal. Froebel at once wrote to Von Raumer explaining the error, and showing that his Kindergarten system had nothing whatever to do with his nephew Karl's high-school system; and he further explained that it was based on religion and a love of order, and that one of his main objects was to instil in the children's minds a respect for law, whether human or divine ; and that anyone who would take the trouble to enquire into his methods might trace this principle in all that was done ; that his work and his writings were open to the inspection of anyone whom the Government might choose for this duty; and he trusted that in simple justice the Prussian Government would see fit to release him and his educational system from the prohibition they had just issued. But Von Raumer, with blind fanaticism, either did not, or would not, see the truth, and Froebel received the following harsh answer: "Dear Sir,—In answer to yours of the 27th, I beg to say that neither your explanations nor the printed matter you enclose impel me to reconsider the decision I had deliberately arrived at."

The fact is that Froebel's doctrine of free development was very little understood, and led many to regard him as belonging to the revolutionary party in Germany, against which there was at this time a violent reaction. And Karl Froebel's introduction of the Kindergarten system into his girls' school added to the confusion.

Whether the judgment pronounced was true of Karl Froebel's school or not, it was certainly most unjust to one whose persistent aim was union with God, and who affirmed again and again that "All education, to be effectual, must be based upon religion, otherwise it is one-sided and imperfect"; and that "Education consists in promoting the expression of the divine in man."*

All who witnessed the Keilhau festivals or the daily life at Marienthal must have been impressed with the religious tone that characterised all Froebel's undertakings, so that this embittering of his last days by persecution from a religious point of view was certainly as unmerited as it was deplorable. Hitherto Froebel had worked with almost youthful energy and strength. But the suddenness of the blow dealt him by the most powerful of the German States utterly crushed him. He was wounded to the quick to think that, through a mere error, the fruit of his life-long effort should be thus destroyed. Though more than ever convinced of the value of his idea, and of his innocence of the charges made against him by the Prussian Government, he could not help feeling that they should be met and refuted.

Night and day did the old man labour, and many were the friends who came forward to help him. Several articles on the Christian teaching in the

* It is only in freedom that the best and highest in human nature can be developed, *i.e.*, man can only express his highest self in his own peculiar way. It is this noble individuality which marks him off from others. Froebel calls this individuality "the divine in man," in contradistinction to that which he shares with other human beings. He says in *The Education of Man* (Part 2, par. 18): "The Spirit of God is revealed most perfectly when the being of the child is allowed to unfold in accordance with his individuality."

Kindergarten appeared in the periodicals of the time; but Von Raumer remained obdurate. And the strength which had been equal to any amount of propaganda, was no longer sufficient to resist the obstinacy and prejudice that were now opposed to it.*

A few happy days were still in store for him, however, for a Conference had been arranged at Liebenstein for the last days of September, and Froebel was in hope that this would help to keep the true view of his work before the public, and to spread it amongst the women of Germany.†

Diesterweg presided on the first day, 27th September, and gave an account of the several Kindergartens represented by teachers present at the Conference, and of the establishment by the Women's Education Union of the first Kindergarten in Berlin, in connection with the Pestalozzi-house. Herr Georgens next spoke of the Kindergarten he had attached to his normal school for girls at Baden-Baden, and which he declared to be the very root and foundation of his establishment.

The Froebel system had also taken a strong hold in Alsatia, and the Strasburg professors were in hopes that the French Government would send some students

---

* This terrible decree against the Kindergarten, issued on the 7th August, 1851, was not repealed till 1860, too late, alas! to give any consolation to its founder.

† Already, in July, Froebel, Middendorff, Diesterweg, and Rector Köhler, had met *en petite comité* in the drawing-room of one of the Liebenstein guests to discuss the possibility of spreading a more thorough pedagogic insight amongst women, and it had then been decided to discuss the matter in a wider circle. It was thought that the most encouraging thing for Froebel would be to get together as much testimony as possible of the progress and life of the Kindergarten movement up to this point.

to be trained at Marienthal. The Princess of Baden had promised to start a Kindergarten at Neuwied. Next, Marquart, of Dresden, described his adaptation of Kindergarten principles to the teaching of transition and higher classes, and showed what an excellent preparation for the higher grades the Kindergarten was, if carried out as Froebel intended it. Heinrich Hoffmann told the meeting about the three Hamburg Kindergartens; the first started by Alwina Middendorff (now Frau Wichard Lange), the second by Veit, and the third by himself. Middendorff reported on the Keilhau institution, and Froebel on the Liebenstein and Rudolstadt Kindergartens.

Further information as to the spread of the system was contributed by Frauleins Henrietta Breymann, Marie Cræmer, and others, and the following testimony to the excellence of the system was quoted by Froebel as coming from the lips of an old Catholic priest: "The Kindergarten is the result of the purest humanity, and of the most deeply religious Protestantism, and yet those who ought to protect Protestantism want to deprive children of it." With this the morning ended. In the afternoon Froebel gave a lecture on the principles underlying his system; and the proceedings of the first day terminated with an exhibition of gifts and occupations.

A spirited meeting was held on the following day. Amongst the speakers were Rector Koehler, Marquart, Diesterweg, Middendorff, and Frau Froebel. Froebelian methods were discussed from a scientific, a psychological, and pedagogic point of view. Certain objections to the system were refuted by men who were in no way connected with Froebel, but who had formed their judgment on actual experience. In the afternoon Froebel gave demonstrations of gifts and occupations, and directed some games. The pupils of the Liebenstein Kindergarten attended for the purpose, and the merry faces of the children showed their enjoyment. In the evening some carefully-prepared games were gone through with great success by a number of young teachers of both sexes.*

Froebel was the soul of the games, and the happy day was long remembered by those present. One of the visitors compared the scene with the Olympian games, and all saw in this Kindergarten festival a promise of the refining influences of the new education.

A meeting was held on the third day to consider the best means of advancing the Froebel cause. Professor Mueller insisted on the importance of nature studies for women. Finally Froebel was urged to publish an account of his system. Diesterweg proposed that a guide should be issued, and also that well-known educationists in the chief cities of Germany should be induced to take up the subject.

Poesche proposed the starting of a magazine. Middendorff, in advocating the training of women teachers, reminded the audience of the dignified position of woman in ancient times, giving as examples the Vestal Virgins, the Sybils, and the Lowly Maid Divine. At the conclusion of the Conference the following resolutions were put and carried:—1st, "That Friedrich Froebel's contribution to pedagogy is of the utmost importance for the understanding of childhood.

---

* What a pity it is that we have lost sight of Froebel's idea of initiating men as well as women into this excellent work.

His principles are adapted to help mothers and to benefit family life. Hence the Kindergarten movement is worthy of our utmost support, and those who work for it deserve the gratitude of the nation."

The objects of the system were drawn up as follows :—

1. An all-sided development of innate faculty in accordance with the nature of every child.
2. A thorough training of the child's physique; special senses.
3. The promotion of skill in various directions.
4. The training of the moral and religious instincts.
5. A general culture of child nature.

The Conference further expressed its approval of the means adopted by Froebel for attaining his object, *i.e.*, games, singing, gymnastic exercises, nature teaching, drawing, colouring, special Kindergarten gifts and occupations, stories, poems and songs, intercourse with equals and superiors.

This report of the meeting was signed by nineteen of the most prominent educational authorities present.

It was resolved to start a Froebel periodical for the spread of the system, under the editorship of Dr. Bruno Marquart, of Dresden. (The earlier articles were written by Froebel and his immediate disciples.)

The eloquence and power with which Froebel, now in his sixty-ninth year, addressed this vast assembly of educationists, gave little evidence of his approaching end. Certain signs of exhaustion, however, showed themselves to his more intimate friends; and it was a matter of grief to Middendorff that he could not at this time leave Keilhau in order to help his friend work out a complete account of the system. Such a document would no doubt have proved most valuable. As it was, the Froebelians had to content themselves with the recognition they had won from those present at the Conference. Froebel carried away from the meeting a feeling of peace and comfort, and appeared more and more to realise his unity with nature. He said to Middendorff, " I feel our life to have been exceptionally harmonious, and yours and mine will continue to make a complete whole even when we are separated, for if I am the head, you are the heart of this great work."

His health grew more delicate and fragile during the winter and early spring, but he enjoyed the restfulness and harmony of spirit that reigned in his Marienthal home. His young wife was devotion itself, and the students who formed part of the family circle vied with each other in anticipating the wishes of the dear "Master." " It is a great consolation to me," Froebel's wife wrote later, "that during his last autumn and winter Froebel saw exemplified in his little circle his idea of unity of life."

It is an old saying that to each comes his happiest day and his end. Froebel's happiest day, perhaps, was his seventieth birthday (21st April, 1852). His students had planned a suitable celebration in his honour, and fortunately Middendorff was able to come and direct them. He best knew how to infuse into the songs, games, and other proceedings the spirit of his friend.

Froebel was awakened at sunrise by the fresh voices of students singing a carol, and on rising he was led into a room charmingly decorated with flowers, where the birthday offerings had been tastefully arranged in various parts of the room. Amongst these were two pictures: one of Pestalozzi and his orphan children, at Stanz, the other of the Madonna, with a poem by Middendorff. Frau Froebel had contributed a piece of fine work, and the students an orange tree, to symbolise the development of the human being. The servants brought flowers and birthday wishes. The students were dressed in white, with green wreaths, red roses, and rainbow-coloured streamers. As Froebel entered they greeted him with a part song composed for the occasion:—

> "Sieh uns hier in Vereine,
> Dass die Liebe erscheine
> Zu dem herrlichen Fest,
> Dankbar—wir dich umringen,
> Kindlich—wir all Dich umschlingen;
> Denn ja dein väterlich Herz uns nicht lässt.
> Du hast reich uns beglücket,
> Wie der Lenzeshauch schmücket
> Neubelebend die Flur;
> Segen träufelst Du nieder,
> Freude auf Schwestern und Brüder
> Wie auf die Saaten der himmliche Thau.
> Doch wie bist Du vor allen
> Unsrer Kinder Gefallen
> Ihre Sonne und Luft;
> Liebend zu Dir sie Sehen
> Betend sie mit uns erflehen;
> Vater! Besel'ge und stärk ihm die Brust!"

The meaning of the students' costumes was explained as follows:—The white dresses symbolised the innocence of his Kindergarten children; the rainbow ribbons his first gift; the green wreaths the Kindergarten circle; the roses the bright thoughts and love of children with which he filled their maiden hearts. This celebration gave Froebel a great deal of pleasure, and his friends noticed with thankfulness his quiet confidence and peace of mind. "It was a most impressive occasion," says Middendorff, "and Froebel put a meaning into our efforts and offerings of which we ourselves were only half conscious." He pointed to a baby in its mother's arms as an exemplification of completeness and unity, and he himself was beaming with the peace of age and the joy of youth. A publisher in Weimar had sent him a splendidly illustrated Bible, the Countess of Hessen-Philipsthal a bouquet and congratulations, and in the afternoon the Salzung and Liebenstein Kindergartens played a number of Kindergarten games together.

The postman came laden with letters and presents from Kindergarten teachers working in different places. All expressed grateful affection for the master. Children and teachers joined in songs and tableaux. Finally, at sunset, the students crowned Froebel with a myrtle wreath. And so ended this happy day. Alas, that such rest and contentment should have been disturbed!

Letters and papers from Hamburg brought news of further misunderstandings and strife, that deeply hurt him, and at length he could no longer hide from his wife and Middendorff the pain and suffering they caused him.

"Alas!" he said one morning, "we must not give ourselves up to our innocent joy. We must be up and doing. These accusations must be refuted at once."

Middendorff wished to divert his friend's attention from these troubles, and planned a visit to the Salzung Kindergarten. This device was partially successful, but it was noticed for the first time that instead of participating in the games, Froebel would sit down and look on; also that on his return home he was more quiet than usual. The distress caused by the prohibition of Kindergartens in Prussia, and the opposition from which his work had suffered, at length told upon his wonderful health. His doctor urgently advised him to rest, but could not prevent his starting a long refutation of the recent attacks made upon him, nor could he prevent him from sitting up in bed for days together to make notes of a new training course for the students. At length, however, he was unable longer to withstand the illness that was coming upon him, and after one last climb up the Altenstein, on May-day, and the enjoyment with his friends of "a last sunset," his magnificent energy and health gave way. He revived a little as the days grew warmer, and some of his old brightness and energy seemed to come back. He even accepted Dr. Hoffmann's invitation to the Teachers' Congress to be held at Gotha at Whitsuntide. He was quiet and thoughtful throughout the journey, and went straight to the Conference Hall. He entered during Diesterweg's address, and on his arrival the assembly rose as one man. At the end of the speech he was further welcomed by three cheers proposed by the President. Froebel's contribution to the Conference concerned nature teaching for the young, and he gave many interesting examples of his method and its results. Demonstrations of Kindergarten lessons followed.

Froebel was entertained during the Conference by one who had great sympathy with teachers and with the Kindergarten movement. At the converzazione in the evening he dwelt on the great influence this movement must have on the position of women; also on the necessity for giving every teacher of young children a knowledge of the system. On the whole the Conference was cheering and encouraging, and Froebel was merry and talkative on the way home. At Marienthal he was met by his students, who had decorated the house in honour of his return. He showed his pleasure at this reception, and spent some happy hours with them. But neither the encouragement he had met with at the Conference, nor this welcome home, could make him forget his great sorrow. And though he did his best to disguise it, his sensitive nature had received a wound from which he was not to recover.

On the 6th June he was attacked by the illness which proved fatal. In health he had often been stern and exacting. Now he was remarkably gentle and submissive, and gave a welcome to all. He would talk cheerfully with his wife or his doctor, and would smile and thank the children or students who brought him flowers. Sometimes he would direct the arrangement of them, or he would express his enjoyment of the fresh air coming in through the open window, and then speak of his union with God and nature. Middendorff arrived on the 17th, but was only allowed to see him in the morning. Barop came from Keilhau, and Dr. Clemens from Rudolstadt. He discussed with him the details of his will. Then he asked to have read over to him an old letter from one of his godparents, which he called his "credentials." This was repeated several times.

Middendorff realised how precious to Froebel was his Christian faith. Little as he was accustomed to talk about it, there it evidently lay at the root of his life. He exhorted his friends in Keilhau to live a life of unity and harmony, and entrusted his wife to their

LAST DAYS.   223

care. He begged his doctor to endeavour to interest the local government in his work, and especially the Duchess of Rudolstadt. "It is Christian work," he said; "my endeavour has been to make Christianity a reality."

"No one can doubt that," answered the doctor.

He then asked his students to sing him a lullaby; and the next day (Saturday evening) he bid adieu to a lady friend, who had zealously worked for him in Liebenstein (Frau Pietzsch). He also bade farewell to his faithful friend Middendorff, thanking him again and again for his sympathy. On Sunday he was weaker, and tried in vain to press to his lips the hand of a little child who had brought him a dove. In the night he asked for wine, and Middendorff administered the Communion.

At about seven o'clock in the evening of the Monday he desired to be propped up in a sitting position, and his eyes opened once more on the face of his friend Middendorff; then closed for ever. All present sank on their knees (his wife, Middendorff, Frau Marquart, and a nurse were present), with the feeling almost as if they had seen a beloved child go to sleep. "Nature," said Middendorff, "made her last effort and then was still. The mind went peacefully, lovingly, thankfully back to its source. A life harmonious, pure, and true in all directions was closed. He was himself a representation of his beloved sunset; the light of his being set upon us like the sun; and I felt as if, like the sun, he must return to us. Even in my sorrow I realised the eternity of life, and that one day death and weeping will be no more. His thoughts had often led him to the light, and now had come the time when he should penetrate into a new day. He who had stood so near to Nature, who had listened for her words, and followed her law in simple trust, now lay on her breast like a loving child. Surely she would reward his love. He was her faithful son, and she his true mother. And thus she took him to herself."

With flowers about him he lay as if soothed to rest by the tones of the men's voices singing the funeral hymn. He was buried on the 24th June, in the picturesque little churchyard of Schweina, about a mile from Marienthal. An immense procession of friends, adults and children followed him to the grave. The funeral oration was pronounced by Pastor Rueckert, who, after alluding to Froebel's work for women, for children, and for humanity, concluded with the following words:—"Here lies a noble heart, resting from its labours. Froebel's work was for the good of earliest childhood and latest posterity. He hoped, and his hope was not in vain." Middendorff wound up with a short address in praise of his friend, and all dispersed.*

Middendorff arranged his monument in the form of a column, made with cube, cylinder, and ball. Goethe's words, "Come let us live for our children," were inscribed upon it.

"Froebel's last word," wrote Dr. Wichard Lange, "has gone with him to the grave; it will be difficult for his disciples to complete his work; they will require well-sustained and patient effort. How many questions had we on our lips for the dear master, and

* See MADAME DE MARENHOLZ' *Die Arbeit und die neue Erziehung*, p. 559, and *Froebel's Ausgang aus dem Leben*, by MIDDENDORFF.

how I looked forward to a quiet week in the autumn, alone with him, away from all disturbance. Now, alas! all I have is remembrance, unless I can come to see you (Middendorff) at Marienthal. You are right in saying that work is the best consolation; it will now be a matter of honour for his disciples to show themselves brave in his work."

Diesterweg says that Froebel's treatment of education from a scientist's point of view, *i.e.*, as a natural process, an evolution, places him amongst originators and pioneers in the educational world; and no less original does he find it for old age practically to concern itself with the activities characteristic of infants. Old people are, as a rule, he says, apt to shun the unrest of childhood, and to content themselves with theories about it. Froebel, however, in his zeal for the right treatment of the little ones, joined in their games with a happy unconcern, that, like his great contemporary Pestalozzi, he was often called "crazy" and "old fool." He shared, too, Pestalozzi's profound educational instincts and his simplicity and honesty of nature. Both these great men were impelled by a love of humanity to devote themselves to the common good. Both had a rare insight into human nature, and, at the same time, a peculiar liability to be deceived by the individual.

Blochmann says of Pestalozzi: "This wise philosopher, who knew childhood so well, little understood men, nor the cultivated barbarism of his time."

Mr. Hanschmann compares Froebel's chief intellectual and practical support to Pestalozzi's (*i.e.* Middendorff and Barop to Niederer and Schmidt.)

But here Froebel certainly had the advantage, for

Q

the loyalty of his friends was as unique as it was admirable. Indeed, Froebel was very happy in all his domestic relations. His family and intimate friends were devoted to him, and the circle at Keilhau was like an extended family. Froebel's eldest brother was, until death parted them, his best friend, whilst Christian Froebel devoted his hardly-earned means to the carrying out of his brother's idea. Amongst the practical good deeds of Froebel we may note the excellent education he gave his own nephews and that which he provided for the two descendants of the Luther family, whose parents could not afford to educate them.

There is a fundamental difference, however, in the starting-point of these two educationists. Pestalozzi's experience had produced in him a keen sense of the perversity of the human heart and a deep compassion for the suffering it entailed. His one desire was to lead men to believe in goodness. Froebel, on the other hand, sees in every infant a possible "perfection of humanity," and in every maiden "a future Madonna." He assumes the inherent goodness of human nature,* and in the possibility of bringing about a natural development of the human being entirely in the direction of goodness.† Having no children of his own, all children claimed his affectionate care. Love of humanity, and especially of childhood, was his most prominent feature. He would go out of his way to

---

* The primary impulses of nature are always right; there is no native perversity in the human heart.—J. J. ROUSSEAU.

† This sunny aspect of human nature gives to the Froebel system a brightness and a cheerfulness which are pre-eminently in harmony with the joyousness and elasticity of childhood.

meet a child, and look into its wide-open eyes, in which, he said, he read "à promise of heaven."

We have in Froebel's own words* a comparison between his own attitude towards education and that of Pestalozzi. "Just as Pestalozzi," he says, "makes 'Home-education' (*Wohnstubenkraft*) his central point, I adopt as my main principle the harmonising of life (*allseitige Lebeneinigung*), *i.e.*, the adaptation of the child's education to his various relationships. I would follow nature by giving scope to all the powers of the human being, so that there might be a harmonious growth of the whole being similar to that of the seedcorn or tiny plant."

Froebel liked to regard the Kindergarten in Germany as a memorial to Gutenberg, the inventor of the art which has done so much for the spread of education. His work in Switzerland may be taken as a tribute to the greatest educator of modern times; whilst his happy circle at Marienthal is an exemplification of his love of humanity.

* In the *Wochenschrift*.

CHAPTER XII.

FROEBEL'S IMMEDIATE SUCCESSORS.

1852 TO 1874.

Middendorff's Death—His Successors in the Froebel Propaganda—The Kindergarten Movement in Germany, France, Belgium, Austria, Italy, and England.

MIDDENDORFF'S one wish and endeavour after the death of his friend was to see his work established on a solid basis; and to be, as far as lay in his power, a second Froebel. "Now comes my turn to be born," he said, and straight away set himself to pick up as many as possible of the threads of his friend's work. With the work, alas, for which he never thought he could do enough, he inherited his friend's anxieties, responsibilities, and troubles, and these, with the incessant effort they entailed, told upon his health, which had hitherto been good. His first care was to complete the training course which Froebel left unfinished at Marienthal. But his own work at Keilhau prevented his taking up his abode there, and it was eventually decided to make certain additions to the building of the mother institution, and carry the Marienthal students thither. The students have much to say on the charm and thoroughness of Middendorff's teaching. The Keilhau community were keenly alive to the necessity of sending out as many well-trained and competent Kindergarten teachers as possible.

On Sunday afternoons Middendorff played Kindergarten games with children of all ages from the neighbouring village of Schweina. Many a mother would stand watching with delight the happy faces of the children, as they moved hither and thither under the direction of this kindly, lovable philanthropist, whose countenance "beamed with the noble thoughts that filled his heart."

Middendorff was invited to represent the Kindergarten cause at the Fifth National Conference of Teachers, to be held in May of this year (1852), at Salzung, close to the scene of Froebel's latest labours. The opening address on the "Nature, Object, and Effect on Education generally of the Kindergarten Movement," was delivered by Dr. Schulze, who reminded the audience of Froebel's presence at the previous Conference at Gotha, and dealt with certain prejudices against the system on the part of parents and teachers who had not taken the trouble to inform themselves of its true nature. He appealed to those present, who had had any opportunity of judging of the matter, to testify to the effect of the system on their children's conduct, character, and general intelligence. As to their religious training, he would only refer enquirers to those who knew Froebel in private life, and who had seen his teaching in the Kindergarten. Such friends could not doubt of his truly Christian and religious spirit. Middendorff spoke next, and Diesterweg, who was present, reports upon his evident grasp of the subject, and his remarkably clear exposition. Many, indeed, held that as a teacher and expounder of the system Middendorff surpassed its founder. As the fellow-worker and fellow-sufferer of Froebel, he regarded himself as the natural representative of his system, and the Kindergarten as a sacred trust, to which it was impossible to do too much honour. Froebel had done good service to teachers in handing to them this natural system of training of the young child, and this service had been publicly acknowledged in his presence at the last Conference at Gotha, where the Froebel cause had been declared to be the cause of all teachers. It only remained for him to dwell upon one or two of the central principles on which the Kindergarten was based. In Pestalozzi's country, where the doctrine of educating the child from the cradle had taken root, Froebel's early education of the child had found a ready welcome, and it was in this land of freedom that many of the details of his system had been worked out. Froebel's discovery of *spontaneity* as the starting-point in the child's education was the keystone of the system. Froebel himself had felt that his task was completed: "Now," he had said, "I can die, for the idea is born!"

But this principle of spontaneity, self-activity, and self-reliance on the part of the little child, implied in the educator not only a knowledge of childhood, with its varying phases, but a careful study of the individual child; in short, a study of the human being at every stage of his existence. Froebel's system aimed at training the whole child* with due regard to childhood in general. It provided occupations for

---

* Pestalozzi claimed as the right of every human being, the training of his faculties.

him in harmony with his tendencies and capabilities; occupations which could be pursued peacefully, undisturbedly, and in the child's own way; occupations which were adapted to inspire the little child with a love of work, and to prepare him for his later duties.* The heart and soul of Kindergarten education is a productive self-activity for the good of others, an all-round expression of child-mind, and a fair chance for the individual.

He further insisted that the child should be allowed to work in his own way. Froebel's gifts and occupations were so adapted to child-nature that they induced in the children a love of work for work's sake. They formed a bond between home and school duties. The child has within him every condition for his development as a complete, self-dependent creature, able to fulfil perfectly his obligations to his fellow-man, to nature, and to God. Some of the audience saw no necessity for an institution whose purpose it was to mediate between the home and the school, but the Conference ended by passing the following resolution:—" That this system is *true to child-nature* is evident from the happiness of the children under its influence; that it is *practical* is seen by the use it makes of the child's innate tendencies, and the love of work which it engenders. Finally this love of work, and the training which the Kindergarten provides in observation, skilfulness, and general intelligence, renders it *a valuable and excellent preparation for school life.*"†

---

* This was an excellent answer to those who were accustomed to look upon school children as so many brains to be crammed.

† "Be strong that you may be serviceable."

After the Conference Middendorff gave himself up to the enjoyment of his beloved Thuringian forest, which was always a refreshment and delight to him. Many an inspiration came to him amidst the beauty of his native hills. In October he attended a National Festival at Darmstadt, in commemoration of the throwing off of the French yoke. He returned to his work with renewed strength. He loved the winter time, and watched with delight the first falling snowflakes on the 26th November. Looking at the vast white expanse before him, he said to his wife, "How I love the snow. Does it not look as if nature were dead? And yet what teeming life is covered by that white pall! So it is with life." It was with difficulty that he tore himself from the beautiful sight. But the children wanted him, and after playing with them and holding a short discourse on "immortality," he retired to rest. This was Middendorff's last day on earth, for during the night following upon it he was seized with paralysis, due to the incessant labour and struggle he had gone through in his endeavour to compass the noble objects he shared with his friend. Diesterweg says: "Middendorff was truth, candour, and fidelity personified, and had a well-balanced mind. His gifts, his nature, and personality leave many a loving memory in the hearts of his friends."

Middendorff's sudden death left Froebel's widow once more alone. The teachers at Keilhau were too busy to help her. Had Dresden been favourable to the Kindergarten system she would have liked to settle there. In the autumn of 1854, however, the principal of the higher grade Kindergarten in Hamburg applied to her for a teacher, and she offered to take one of her students thither and start her in the work. Her offer was accepted, and she found in Hamburg such an ample outlet for her educational efforts that she soon had a Kindergarten and training school of her own, together with transition and preparatory classes.

She also organised the first Kindergarten in Berlin, under the management of two of Froebel's best pupils, and, with Diesterweg, founded a Kindergarten Union, of which she became the president.

Whilst Froebel's work was being thus successfully carried out in Hamburg by his widow, another woman, perhaps the most able and *influential exponent* of his work, was busy elsewhere. This was the Baroness of Marenholtz-Bülow. It was she who now stepped forth, and, in her turn, picked up the threads of the Froebel work.

It was as if she, too, like Middendorff, had said to herself, "Now it is *your* turn to be born." Frau von Marenholtz thoroughly understood Froebel's pedagogic idea. She was a woman of influence, able to express herself in several languages, and gifted with a pleasing manner. Hence she was able to win over to the cause many whom perhaps even Middendorff would have been unable to reach. She worked zealously in Berlin during the winter of 1851-52, and succeeded in starting a Kindergarten,* and with Diesterweg's support a Kindergarten Union. After the death of her son, in 1853, this accomplished lady devoted herself entirely to the Froebel propaganda. She proceeded to London in 1854, and started several

* This Kindergarten, under Frl. Erdmann, like the one at Erfurt, survived in spite of the State prohibition.

Kindergartens, which attracted a certain amount of public attention. Amongst those who were favourable to the system in England was Charles Dickens.

In January, 1855, Frau von Marenholtz went to Paris, where she delivered over one hundred lectures, and succeeded in bringing about a reform in the infant schools or *Salles d'asyle*. The followers of Fourier were especially interested in her efforts. The Empress Eugénie was induced to become President of the Central Committee of the *Salles d'asyle;* and Frau von Marenholtz was invited, by the Minister of Education, to give some demonstrations. This she did in the normal school of Madame Pape Carpentier. In 1856 Madame A. Köchlin started a Froebel infant school in the Rue de la Pépinière, on which occasion M. A. Coquerel, the well-known Protestant minister, gave the opening address. This Kindergarten was to admit children of Catholic and Jewish parents as well as Protestants.

Amongst people of influence in Paris who supported Frau von Marenholtz in her propaganda were M. Richard Gardon (editor of a paper entitled *La Science des Mères*); the philanthropist, Jules Mallet; M. Auguste Comte, and the Archbishop of Paris. The Abbé Le Noir, too, helped to translate the *Koselieder* into French.

Frau von Marenholtz put Froebel's *Education of Man* into the hands of all who were likely to spread the idea. M. Jacobs' *Manuel Pratique du Jardin d'Enfants* was compiled under her direction, Frls. Breymann and Chevallier, and Madame Ruelens, contributing different parts. Frl. Henrietta Breymann gave the Brussels students a course of instruction in

Kindergarten occupations, whilst Frl. Chevallier took a class of nuns for the same purpose. Mlle. Masson assisted Frau von Marenholtz in starting the Kindergarten system in Belgium.

Frau von Marenholtz's lectures were a great success everywhere, and by her tact and intelligence she always won the support of the authorities. M. J. Coune, of Antwerp; Ch. Hofmann, of Ghent; and M. Tiberghien, a disciple of Krause, did everything to support her, and the little town of St. Josse-ten-Noode sent her a memorial in recognition of her work. In 1859 she and Madame Köchlin established a Kindergarten Association at Mulouse, in Alsatia. In 1860, she went to Switzerland, delivering lectures at Lausanne, Geneva, Neuchatel, Berne, and Zurich. Here she won the friendship and adherence of Professor Raoux. Many Swiss friends were won over to the cause at the Conference which took place at Berne in the following year.*

In 1861 Frau von Marenholtz took up her abode in Berlin, and directed all her efforts towards removing the restrictions from which the Kindergarten movement suffered in Prussia. She induced the Women's Union, of which she was president, to start two good Kindergartens under the direction of Frls. Krueger and Ida Seele. And it was by dint of her perseverance and energy that the People's Kindergarten was founded. She also persuaded Professor Carl Schmidt† to start a paper called the *Erziehung der Gegenwart*, for the elucidation of the principles. The first article,

---

* The highest success was won for the Kindergarten system in Switzerland, in 1864, by the combined efforts of Henrietta Breymann and Madame de Portugall. See Appendix II.

† Unfortunately this able man died in 1864.

"The Educational Requirements of Modern Times," was written by Frau von Marenholtz. In it she proposed the application of the system to the lower forms of the school. In 1863 she founded an "Association for Home Education in Berlin." The main objects of this are explained in her book, entitled *Work and the New Education according to Froebel*. This association gave rise to seven Kindergartens, a training school for teachers, and a school for girls. During Frau von Marenholtz's stay in Berlin, no less than three hundred students passed through her hands. In 1867 the beautiful grounds of the Thier-Garten were opened for games. This movement was supported by Professor Virchow and other influential persons.

She spent the summer of 1867 travelling about for her health, and doing what she could for the spread of the system. Her demonstrations in Munich, Cassel, and Dresden made many converts, and it was her influence that gave rise to the publication of the Italian journal, *L'Educazione Moderna*, and to the normal school for Kindergarten teachers established at Venice under Mlle. Levi.

The Austrian Government was the first to acknowledge the Kindergarten as an essential part of the national educational scheme. Inspired first by Fichte and afterwards by Frau von Marenholtz, during her stay at Liebenstein, Dr. Hoerfarter rendered excellent service to the cause, and was the means of establishing in the year 1872 a Kindergarten normal school at Kuffstein.

In the winter 1871-1872 Frau von Marenholtz delivered a course of lectures in Venice and in Florence, where the municipality started a most successful

Kindergarten. The system was applied in Rome in a school for the poor; whilst at Naples a people's Kindergarten was established by the energy of Frau Salis Schwabe. The funds for this were provided partly by the Italian Government and partly by English liberality.*

The Kindergarten system lost in 1871 two excellent exponents: Thekla Naveau (1822-1871), a pupil of Middendorff, and the author of *Stories for the Home and the Kindergarten;* and Wilhelmine Marquart, who studied with Froebel, and conducted a Kindergarten in connection with her husband's school in Dresden. Frau Marquart possessed qualities which enabled her to assimilate in a peculiar way Froebel's and Middendorff's teaching, and to enter thoroughly into the spirit of her husband's work. She trained many excellent Kindergarten teachers. Amongst the most vigorous workers for Froebel we must not forget to mention Rudolf Benfey, of Berlin, who contributed much to the spread of clear ideas about the Kindergarten; and Heinrich August Koehler, of Gotha, who became a convert to the Froebel teaching at the Gotha Conference in 1852, and who is the best-known representative of the Froebel cause in Europe.

He began with a private class for the education of his own children, and was soon at the head of an excellent training school for Kindergarten teachers. It was he who was invited by the Russian Government to represent the Kindergarten cause, both on the occasion of their two-hundredth anniversary of Peter the Great's birthday, and also at the Polytechnic Exhibition at

* It is to the energy and enthusiasm of this lady that we owe the existence of the Froebel Institute in London.

Moscow in 1873. He was part editor of a paper called *Kindergarten and Elementary Classes*, which, as the mouthpiece of the German Froebel Association, has done so much to spread an intelligent understanding of the system. In this paper Koehler treats of the earliest stages of education; whilst Frau von Marenholtz in her article deals with education generally.

The new education, with the necessary modification of school life, is now looked forward to by many with hope and confidence. Richard Waldeck, who had made Froebel's acquaintance in 1851, says: "As the gentle breath of spring passes over the earth, leaving riches in its train, so the Kindergarten system carries with it, as it spreads through the world, innocence and joy.

"Surely we may look forward to a day when Froebel's unity and harmony of life shall take the place of the one-sided intellectual development of the school, and the inefficient education of the solitary child,* when the human being will be trained to work in peace and freedom with others, *i.e.*, to form part of a community of light and love. The beneficent movement started at Keilhau and Blankenburg, in the Thuringian Forest, will in time, no doubt, spread to all civilized countries; will bring about the social, educational, and religious reforms that are needed for man's happiness and development. The day is surely coming when a brighter sun will shine over a happier earth, banishing the old habits of passion and vice, and reviving the simplicity of the golden age; when the strength of manhood and the innocence of childhood shall be united, when the world shall be a Kindergarten, and the happy children playing therein humanity."

* In home education the learner is, of necessity, practically alone.

APPENDIX I.

FROEBEL'S "EDUCATION OF MAN."

FROEBEL'S *Education of Man*, published in 1826, gives not so much a complete system of education as a *résumé* of the contents of his smaller publications from the year 1820, including his scheme for the school at Helba. This putting into shape of his thought and experience was probably the immediate result of Froebel's acquaintance with the works of Krause, which greatly interested him.

The first Kindergarten was not started till ten years later, but the germs of the Kindergarten system are seen both in the Helba scheme and in the principles enunciated in the *Education of Man*.

Froebel's education is entirely based upon the idea of unity with God, or the conscious development of the "Divine in man." He explains this as something which is inherent in the individual and peculiar to him. Fichte calls it man's "genius" or individuality.

Froebel says: "The destiny of the human being is to become conscious of his spiritual nature and to reveal it in his life," *i.e.*, to manifest the eternal in the temporal, the infinite in the finite, the heavenly in the earthly, the divine in the human, and "the purpose of education is to assist him to do this consciously, resolutely, and freely." The home is the cradle of spiritual life, and should awaken in man the consciousness of his three-fold nature, and of the relationships this implies (*i.e.*, to nature, man, and God). School and home should co-operate in the development of the religious sense more or less inherent in every child. He should be assisted to express his aspirations and his feeling for union with God, who is first revealed to him through humanity.

Froebel was not alone in the view that every human being must be complete in himself. He can only attain to this completion and perfection through the development of all his powers. It is the whole child that has to be educated. Neither brain nor heart, nor body, nor spirit, makes the child, but all combined. And it is the neglect to provide for his diverse tendencies and powers (or maybe an arbitrary interference with their natural development) which produces such childish faults as idleness, heedlessness, and untruthfulness. *Chaque qualité a ses défauts.* We must be true to nature, whose processes are slow and gradual.*

The view of the universe and of man's place in it which had dominated all philosophy since Schelling's time, naturally underlay Froebel's views on education. Man and nature have the same origin, and are subject to the same laws.

Goethe has said, "Let us live for our children." Froebel adds, "Let us learn our children, learn to know their nature."

The educator should be one who makes a special study of man and of the characteristics and possibilities of childhood. He must take as his guide the natural tendencies and instincts of childhood, which, in Froebel's opinion, are right and good. The child must develop freely and naturally, and must have full scope for these tendencies. Education must follow, not lead; must give and take; must be mobile, yet firm; must act and suffer: for somewhere between these two attitudes lies the good and the true, to which both educator and learner submit. On the patient watchfulness

---

* "The young mind," says Sailer, "has to pass step by step from clearness to distinctness, and from distinctness to comprehension," and he bids us take pattern by the trees, which, he says, "present in turn soft foliage, bud, blossom, seed-vessel, and finally ripe fruit."

of the educator will depend the manifestation of the child's true nature, and the development of the highest and best within him.

It is the child's nature to be restless, active, sportive, imaginative, and productive. He has an aptitude for taking in simple ideas of form, number, colour, size, symmetry, and order. He is remarkably open to the influence of music, poetry, story, and legend; and welcomes almost any occupation for hand and eye that enables him to feel he is sharing in the activities of others.* Here, then, are distinct indications for the guidance of the educator. True education promotes intelligent activity from the first, and this in its turn leads to knowledge. Knowledge and expression amplify and complete each other. We only truly know that which we can clearly express. It is only through sense that we are enabled to learn to understand our surroundings in the world and in nature. Objects are the child's first education, but it is only very gradually that they stand out clearly, one by one, to his hitherto blurred vision. His consciousness of these objects is at first expressed by action. In action thought takes shape, the invisible becomes visible. It is the purpose of education to make the knowledge thus gained more thorough and comprehensive than it would otherwise be, and to enable us to apply it to the needs of life.

The child's *spontaneous self-activity* is at first without object and aimless, but it soon takes the form of sport or play. This tendency is due to an urgent need for self-expression. Speech and play soon become the elements in which he spontaneously manifests his nature, and at the same time the stage of development he has reached. The young child's love of activity must not be confounded with the same quality in the adult, who labours to earn his living or to satisfy his ambition. The grown man works of

---

* Too often, alas! children are trained to physical and mental sloth, whereby an untold wealth of capacity and skill is lost to humanity.

a set purpose to effect an object; the child is impelled to exercise his powers, on the other hand, by an unconscious need to uncloak himself. He does not live "by bread alone," he must move, produce, verify, construct, invent and create. The mind of man, like the mind of God, loves to shape the chaotic and unformed, and this is the meaning of work. In work we resemble our Maker. By labour we inherit the kingdom of heaven. Just as early religious training is important for the child, so is the training to industry. Each helps the other. Religion without work becomes a dream, and work without religion is evil. Froebel says that part of every school day should be devoted to productive work.

The child's surroundings stimulate his will and energy, which are brought to bear upon them with a view to knowledge. Learning and doing with him go hand in hand. It is only by doing that he knows whether he knows.

Fichte also maintained that the learner can only call his own that which he has acquired by his own activity.

> "Wouldst thou possess thy heritage,
> By active use e'en render it thine own ;
> What we employ not but impedes the way,
> What it brings forth the hour can use alone."
> Miss SWANWICK's translation of *Faust*.

"It is by action," says Froebel, "that the child makes the inner outer and the outer inner," *i.e.*, action transforms impression into expression, and in its turn expression emphasises impression. By observation and "Anschauung" he receives ideas, by action he expresses them. Self-expression, or what Froebel calls "Darstellung," is the Alpha and Omega of his system.

The child's earnest and vigorous effort to express himself, which we call play, is no more like the play or pastime of the adult than is his ceaseless and irrepressible activity like the labour of the adult. Parents must beware of treating it as "trifling" and "idling." It is, on the contrary, a manifestation to be valued and encouraged to the utmost. Check the expression of this inner life in the child, and you may do him untold injury; utilise it, and you will find ready to your hand the germs of industry, thrift and order, and of every virtue.

"The sportiveness and joyousness of childhood," says Froebel, "are not to be disdained. The child who plays in a hearty and persevering way until he is exhausted, promises to become a thorough, conscientious man, willing to take his share of the responsibilities of life." Nothing gives the child so full an opportunity of self-expression as his games. In no other occupation is there so much scope for the exercise of limb, sense, voice, and ear; in no other exercise can he so easily manifest his imagination, sense of beauty, social instinct, and spiritual nature. Here, and here alone, he is a complete and all-sided creature.

A good mother has an instinctive appreciation of her child's desire to express himself in a variety of ways; and her ingenuity and inventive power are ever at his service. Froebel's *Mutter-und Kose-Lieder* are based upon the mother's instinctive training. She alone understands his intense earnestness; she alone has the patience and insight necessary to help him.

Froebel wishes to see this instinctive perception of truth on the mother's part transformed into a conscious power of training her child in a systematic and organised way. The motto heading his game of the "Weathercock" gives us a clue as to his meaning:

> "If your child's to understand
> Action in the world without,
> You must let his tiny hand
> Imitate and move about."

The child's development with Froebel forms a continuous whole. There is no line of demarcation between infancy, childhood, youth, and manhood; and when education interferes with this gradual development for the sake of some special training, for which as yet the being is unready, the general growth is impeded. What the developing creature wants is time to become as complete at each stage of growth as possible, so that each succeeding stage may be like a perfect shoot from a perfect bud.

> " Tiny buds their secrets holding
> Soon reveal them silently ;
> Growth is ever an unfolding,
> In the germ the whole doth lie.
> Little blossoms upward tending,
> Spreading out towards the sun,
> Show the road that we must follow ;
> Nature's processes are one." *

> * "Alles ist im Keim enthalten,
> Alles Wachsthum ein Entfalten,
> Leises Auseinanderrücken,
> Dass sich einzeln könne schmücken,
> Was zusammen war gewoben ;
> Wie am Stengel stets nach oben
> Blüt' um Blüte rücket weiter,
> Sieh es an und lern so heiter,
> Zu entwickeln, zu entfalten,
> Was im Herzen ist enthalten."—RUECKERT.

APPENDIX II.

MADAME DE PORTUGALL.

WE are glad to be able to quote a short account of Madame de Portugall's life and work, which appeared in the *Queen* of August 26th :—

"The Baroness Adèle de Portugall, who is for a few weeks in England, is well known, both among educational circles in this country and on the Continent, as the principal of the training college and Kindergarten established by Mrs. Salis Schwabe at Naples—an institution which it is hoped may, by the generosity of its foundress, shortly have its counterpart in England. Madame de Portugall, *née* Homburg, was born in Kœnigsberg, in East Prussia, April 30th, 1828. Her father was an officer in the Prussian army, and Madame de Portugall was educated at home, being early trained by her mother in all domestic duties. When twenty-three she married Baron de Portugall, a retired officer, and they resided on his estate, actively engaged in its management, until the death of the Baron in 1858. Madame de Portugall then threw herself into useful work, in order to relieve the deep sorrow of her bereavement.

"In 1859 she made the acquaintance of the Baroness de Marenholtz Bülow, a lady in whom still centres the deep admiration and reverence of all those who have from her lips learned the wisdom taught by Friedrich Froebel. She was at once his friend and the apostle of his system, and in 1854 introduced the Kindergarten into England.

"Under this lady Madame de Portugall studied the philosophical as well as the practical side of the system, and she also became acquainted with Mlle. Breymann, Froebel's great-niece, now the well-known Frau Schrader, of the Froebel-Pestalozzi House of Berlin. In the spring of 1860 Madame de Portugall came to Manchester and took the direction of Miss Fretwell's Kindergarten. Returning to the Continent in 1862, she again helped Madame de Marenholtz in her work. In the next winter she made the acquaintance of Madame Marenholtz's pupil, Madame Michaelis. A Kindergarten having been started at Geneva, through the interest awakened there by Madame de Marenholtz, Madame de Portugall, when on a holiday trip to that town in search of rest, threw herself at once into the philanthropic work connected with the organisation of this Kindergarten. The holiday trip extended from 1864 to 1873, when she and her energetic friend, Mlle. Progler, were forced to resign in order to have the rest ordered nine years previously.

"In 1876 Madame de Portugall was recalled by the Education Department of Geneva from Mühlhausen (where she had been asked to take up work) to organise the system of Kindergarten teaching in infant schools throughout the canton. Her organisation was triumphantly successful, and overcame the natural resistance of old-fashioned teachers and of the whole bureaucracy of education. When, in 1884, the declining health of Mlle. Progler determined Madame de Portugall to seek for her friend and collaborateur a more genial climate, Madame Schwabe rejoiced in the opportunity which gave to her institution at Naples the principal who carried with her success wherever she went. The result has ratified the choice, and Madame de Portugall labours, as she has ever laboured, not merely to make a Kindergarten, but in the Kindergarten to raise true and noble lives; to gather round her children and teachers who shall hand down to future generations not mere knowledge, but the torch of progress, moral, spiritual, and intellectual. To make good citizens is a higher aim than to make prize-taking scholars, and it is an aim which is much neglected in English pedagogy of to-day."—From *Child Life*, September, 1892 (by kind permission of Messrs. Newman & Co.).

This little notice is far from doing justice to the original genius of Madame de Portugall. Nevertheless, it is valuable as a small contribution towards the history of the Froebel movement. It has long been my wish to give some account of the chief women workers in the Froebel cause. Their excellent work is not known as it should be, and I am sure that the study of such efforts as those of Frau Froebel, Madame de Marenholtz, Frl. Doreck, Frl. Heerwart, Miss Emily Shirreff, Miss Manning, Frau Salis Schwabe, Frau Schrader, Frau Johanna Goldschmid, Madame Michaelis, and many more, would be most profitable reading for those whose way is made easier by their efforts.

INDEX OF NAMES

Ackermark : 24
Ahrens : 109, 113, 171
Alexandrine of Prussia, Princess : 144
Altenstein : 200 sqq., 221
„ Freiherr Von : 42
Amrhyn : 132
"Anschauung" : 27 (n.), 63, 109, 117, 136
Aristotle : 144
Arndt : 22, 33

Bacon, Francis : 63
Baden-Baden : 214
„ Princess of : 215
Bamberg : 21-2
Barop : 97 (n.), 100, 104, 107, 114, 126-7, 129 sqq., 134, 147, 161, 222
Basedow : 62, 81
Benfey, Rudolf : 202, 206-7
Bergmann : 60 (n.)
Berlin : 61, 68-71, 127-8, 143, 144, 182 (n.), 209-10, 235
Berne : 55, 132, 133, 235
Bernhardt, F. : 193
Black : 60 (n.)
„ Forest : 99
Blankenburg : 146, 157 sqq.
Blochmann : 47, 148, 225
Blumenbach : 56 (n.)
Boie : 56
Bormann, K. : 209-10
Brechten : 75
Breslau : 66
Breymann, Henrietta : 182, 234
Brougham, Lord : 144
Bruno, Giordano : 21
Brunswick, Countess of : 150 (n.)
Brussels : 182
Buchanan, James : 144

Bülow, Marenholtz—*vide* Marenholtz.
Burgdorf : 26, 27, 133 sqq., 137, 138, 139, 142
Busch, Frl. : 186

Campe : 62, 85
Carpentier, Mme. : 234
Cavendish : 60 (n.)
Chasseral : 45
Chevallier, Frl. : 234
Chevé System : 30 (n.)
Clemens, Dr. : 222
Coburg : 170
Comenius : 63, 81, 108-9, 112 (n.), 138
Comte, Auguste : 234
Coune, J. : 235
Coquerel, A. : 234-5
Craemer, Marie : 215
"Crèches" : 143-5
Crispine, Ernestine : 95

Dahlenkampf, Frl. : 186
Dalton, John : 60 (n.)
Darmstadt : 144, 152, 174, 232
"Darstellung" : 117-8, 136, 146, 168, 177, 242
Davy : 60 (n.)
De Portugall, Mme. : 245-7
Detnold : 144
Devonshire, Duke of : 144
Dewitz, Herr Von : 21-3.
Dickens, Charles : 234
Diesterweg, Adolph : 188 sqq., 209, 214 (and n.), 215, 221, 225, 229, 232
Doerffling (publisher) : 149-51.
Doreck, Frl. : 247
Dresden : 66, 147, 155-6, 179, 185-6, 237

Duesseldorf: 68

Eddigehausen: 108, 128
Edinburgh: 99
Eichfeld: 83, 102, 179
Eisenach, 159, 170
Eisenberg: 150
Elba, Napoleon's Escape from: 70
Elbe, River: 67
,, Valley: 180
Elizabeth of Prussia: 143
Emme Valley: 134
Erdmann, Frau: 233 (n.)
Erfurt: 233 (n.)
Eugenie, Empress: 234

Fellenberg: 29, 133
Fichte, J. G.: 41, 61 (n.), 65, 67, 81-2, 124-5, 192, 236, 239
Florence, 236
Foelsing, Dr. J.: 174
Fourier: 234
Frankenberg, Adolp: 128, 129, 137, 139 sqq., 147 sqq., 155, 156, 179, 186
Frankenberg Family: 108, 128
,, Luise: 185, 186 (n.)
Frankfort-on-Maine: 23 sqq., 36, 55, 68, 118, 121, 151, 152, 159, 175
Frederick II.: 41
,, William III.: 41
Friedrichsroda: 209
Froebel, August: 3, 5, 14-5
,, Christian: 60, 73-4, 97, 104, 226
,, ,, his children: 97, 102, 107
,, Christoph: 3, 5, 6, 19, 20, 24, 37, 72
,, ,, Mrs.: 73 (n.), 78
,, Elise: 125-6, 132
,, Ferdinand: 73, 98, 122, 129, 141-2
,, Frau Friedrich: 157-8, 167, 215, 247
,, Friedrich Wilh. Aug.: 2
,, Joh. Jac.: 1 sqq., 14-6, 18-9
,, Julius: 72, 76, 99
,, Karl: 72, 77-8, 191, 196-7, 211

Froebel, Theodor: 72
,, Traugott: 3, 16
,, Wilhelm: 72

Gardon, Richard: 234
Gedike: 62
Geneva: 45-6
Georgens: 214
Gerau: 170
Gerstenberg: 12, 15
Girton College: 191 (n.)
Glauchau: 180
Goehrde, Battle of: 68
Goethe: 25, 68, 240
Gloeckner, Bertha: 186
Goldschmid, Frau: 247
Gotha: 221
Göttingen: 22, 33, 55 sqq., 108, 128, 151
Gottling, J. F. A.: 17-8
Griesheim: 24, 72 sqq.
Gross-Goerschen, Battle of:
Gross-Milchow: 21
Gruener, G. A.: 25 sqq., 34, 36-7
Gutenberg: 162
,, Festival: 163

Habig, Pastor: 184-5
Habisch, Emma: 182
Hainberg: 56, 58
Halle: 22, 98, 104, 180
Hamburg: 99, 191 sqq., 197, 232-3
Hammersfeld: 76
Hardenberg, Prince of: 29
Harz Mountains: 60
Havelberg: 68
Heerwart, Frl.: 247
Hegel: 112, 186 (n.)
Heidelberg: 33, 144, 173
"Heimathskunde": 31, 49 (n.)
Helba: 113-5, 118, 239
Herbart, J. F.: 93 (and n.), 154 (n.)
Herder: 58
Hermann, Luise: 179
Herz, Dr.: 186
Herzog, Dr. Karl: 98, 99, 106, 121 (n.), 122, 125
Hessenstein, Countess: 220
Hildburghausen: 21, 170
Hochstaedter, Herr: 159
Hoerfarter, Dr.: 236

INDEX.   251

Hoffmann, Pastor: 6-9, 55, 74
,, Ch.: 235
,, Dr. H.: 215, 221
Hofmeister, Wilhelmine: 94
Hofwyl: 133
Hohnbaum, Dr.: 133   [55, 118
Holzhausen, H. von: 32-3, 36,
Hopf: 29
Humboldt, Alex. von: 56-7, 59 (n.), 60, 63, 68
,, Wilh. von: 56, 61 (n.)
Hungary: 170-1

Ilm—*vide* Stadt-Ilm
Ingelheim: 173
Inselberg: 209

Jacobs: 234
Jahn, Prof. F. L.: 65 *sqq.*
Jena: 13, 14 *sqq.*, 154, 186 (n.)

Kahla: 16
Kaiser, Herr: 149
Kalidasa: 58 (n.)
Kant: 60
Keferstein, Dr.: 186 (n.)
Keilhau: 72, 78, 79 *sqq.*, 125-7, 128, 134, 139, 142, 179, 228
Kell, Julius: 184
Kepler: 18
Kern, Dr.: 159
,, Frau: 170
Klein: 150
Klopstock: 56
Kochler, A.: 214 (n.), 215
,, Rector: 237
Koechlin, Mme.: 234, 235
Koerner, Theodor: 66
Kohl: 177, 186 (n.)
Krause, K. C. F.: 2, 107 *sqq.*, 128, 139 *sqq.*
,, Sidonie: 139, 173
Krueger, Frl.: 235
Kruesi: 29, 48 (n.)
Krug, J. F. Ad.: 51
Kuehne, Gust.: 186, 200
Kufstein: 236

Lange, Dr. Wichard: 30, 75-6, 165, 185, 192, 194, 224-5
Lansdowne, Marquis of: 144
Langethal, Christ.: 75, 77, 89 *sqq.*

Langethal, Heinr.: 66 *sqq.*, 70, 74, 86 *sqq.*, 102, 133, 138, 139, 142, 151
Lavoisier: 60 (n.)
Lawill, Samuel: 9   [186
Leipzig: 147, 149-50, 151, 156,
,, Battle of: 72, 85
Le Noir, Abbé: 234
Leonhardi, H. von: 108-9, 111, 139 *sqq.*, 147-8, 152, 171, 173
Lichtstädt: 83
Liebenstein: 188 *sqq.*, 197, 211 *sqq.*, 216, 236
Lindenare, Von.: 180
Lindner: 149
Loewe, Prof.: 148, 157
Lossius' *Illustrated Bible*: 85
Lucerne: 119, 121, 125 (n.), 126, 129
Luise, Queen: 41
Lussac, Gay: 60 (n.)
Lütkens, Doris: 191, 192
Luther, J. E.: 96-7
,, J. Georg.: 96-7, 98
,, J. Nik.: 96 (n.)
,, Martin: 96
Lützow: 66
Lutzen, Battle of: 68

Macaulay, Mr.: 144
Magdeburg: 180
Maine, River: 32
Mainz: 175
Mallet, Jules: 234
Mann, Friedrich: 47
Mannheim: 144
Manning, Miss: 247
Marenholtz-Bülow, Bertha von: 189, 197, 200, 209, 233 *sqq.*
Marheinecke: 61 (n.)
Marienthal, 188 *sqq.*, 222, 228
Marquart, Bruno: 185-6, 215, 216-7
,, Wilhelmine: 223, 237
Marschner, Aurelia: 186
Masson, Mlle.: 235
Mecklenberg-Strelitz: 21, 22, 41
Meiningen, Duke of: 2, 113-6, 188, 197
Meissen: 186
Michaelis: 98
,, Mme.: 247

INDEX.

Middendorff, Wilhelm : 66 *sqq.*, 70, 74, 75 *sqq.*, 80, 86 *sqq.*, 102, 104, 119, 126, 132-3, 134, 141, 155, 156, 158-9, 161, 172-4, 185, 191-2, 203-4, 214 (n.), 216-20, 222, 223-4, 228 *sqq.*
Middendorff, Alwina : 181, 191, 215
Mont Blanc : 45
Moscow : 238
Mueller, Professor : 216
Muenchenbuchsee : 29
Mulouse : 235
Muralt, Von : 55
Myer (publisher) : 172

Naegeli, G. H.: 51, 119
Naenni : 26
Naples : 237
Napoleon I.: 70
Naveau, Thekla : 237
Neander : 67
Neuchatel : 29, 44, 45
Neuwied : 215
Neuhaus : 10-3
New Lanark : 144
Newnham College : 191 (n.)
"Nibelungenlied": 95
Niebuhr : 61 (n.)
Niederer : 26, 53-4, 55 (n.), 56 *sqq.*
Nikolovius : 41
Novalis : 22-3
Nowosielsky, Theophil : 156

Oberlin, Pastor : 144
Oberweissbach : 1
Orbe, River : 44
Ortaumund : 16
Otto, Prince : 156
Owen, Robert : 144

Parents' Union : 178-9
Paris : 234
,, Peace of [1814]: 68
Pestalozzi : 25, 26, 29, 30, 37, 41 *sqq.*, 64, 81, 114, 134 (n.), 135 *sqq.*, 192, 193-4, 225-6
Peters, Dr.: 147-8
Pfeiffer, M. T.: 51
Pfyffer, E.: 119, 131-2
Pietzsch, Frau : 223

Plamann : 33, 63-4
Plato : 144
Poesche : 216
Priestley : 60 (n.)
Proeschke : 22

Raoux, Professor : 235
Raumer, Von : 211-2, 214
Richter, Jean Paul : 38, 119, 220 (n.)
Ritz, Herr : 186
Rochow, F. E. von : 62
Rome : 237
Rousseau : 30 (n.), 37, 38-9, 62, 81
Rudolstadt, Duke of : 104
,, 68, 79
,, Duchess of : 48, 223
Ruelens, Mme.: 234
Ruete, Dr.: 159
Ruettimann : 119

Saal, Valley of the : 1, 16, 162, 180
Sachsenhausen : 144, 172
Sailer : 38, 240
"Sakontala": 58
Salesie, Frl.: 125 (n.)
Salis-Schwabe, Mme.: 237, 247
"Salles d'Asyle" in Paris : 234
Salomo : 58 (n.)
Salzung : 220, 229
Savigny : 61 (n.)
Savoy : 46
Saxony, Queen of : 155
Schaala : 84
Schaefer : 152
Schaffhausen : 55
Schaffner, Dr.: 97 (n.)
Schaumburg-Lippe, Carol. I. von : 154, 170
Schelling : 21, 186 (n.)
Scheppler, Luise : 144
Schiller : 7
Schimpfer, Karl : 109
Schlegel, Fr.: 58 (n.)
Schleiermacher, F. E., 61 (n.), 67 and (n.), 193
Schliephacke, Dr.: 176
Schmid, Joseph : 54, 55 (n.)
Schmidt, Dr. Carl : 235
,, Professor : 154
Schneider, Karl : 159, 172

INDEX.

Schnyder, Xavier: 119 *sqq.*
Schoenbein, Dr.: 98
Schrader, Dr.: 182 (n.)
Schulze, Dr.: 229
Schwarza: 163
Schwarzburg-Rudolstadt, Carol. L. von: 154, 160
Seele, Ida: 174, 182 (n.), 235
Sempach, Lake of: 119, 126
Seyffarth: 120
Shirreff, Miss: 247
Sondershausen: 170
Sorgau: 180
St. Gothard: 46
St. Josse-ten-Node: 235
Stadt Ilm: 6, 7, 22, 74
Stangenberger: 206
Stein, Freiherr von: 43
Stieler, Frl.: 182
Stollikofer: 4
Stoy, Dr.: 154
Strasburg: 214
Sturm: 4
Stuttgart: 55, 144
Sylvestre de Sacy: 58

Thirty Years' War: 63
Tiberghien: 235
Tillich: 33, 52
Tobler: 29
Traberth, Augusta: 182
,, Julie: 209
Traun, Bertha: 191 (n.)
Tübingen University: 102 (n.)
Tuerk, Chancellor von: 42, 55, 145

Uhlich, Pastor: 180

Unger: 154 (n.)

Valais, Canton: 46
Vauquelin: 60 (n.)
Veit: 215
Venice: 236
Voigt, J. H.: 13, 15, 17-8
Vogel, Dr.: 149, 156-7, 180
Volkstaedt: 94, 163
Voss, J. H.: 56

Wadzeck: 144
Walbach (Alsace): 144
Waldeck, Richard: 238
Warsaw: 156
Wartburg: 25
Wartensee: 119, 120 *sqq.*
Watzum: 182
Weil, Dr.: 159
Weimar: 7
Weiss, Chr. S.: 61 and (n.), 68
Weissenburg, Castle of: 83
Werner, Von: 56 (n.), 61
Westphalia: 75
Willisau: 127, 129 *sqq.*, 133, 134
Winckelmann's "Letters": 19
Wislicenus, Pastor: 180
Wittenberg: 180
Wollweide, Professor: 22
Wuestenfeld, Frau: 191 (n.)

Yverdun: 29, 33, 40-1, 43 *sqq.*

Zeh, Inspector: 99-102, 104, 105, 113.
"Zend-avesta": 19
Ziegenbein: 193

THE SCIENCE AND HISTORY OF EDUCATION.

Beale (A. C.) The Froebel Primer (Reading). 4to, 1s. Three Wall Sheets, ea. 2s. 6d.; or the three unmounted, 3s. 6d.

Bremner (C. S.) The Education of Girls and Women in Great Britain. With a Preface by Miss HUGHES. 4s. 6d.

Bryant (Dr. SOPHIE). Short Studies in Character. 4s. 6d.

Buxton (SYDNEY, M.P.) Over-Pressure and Elementary Education. 1s.

Compayré (Prof. GABRIEL). History of Pedagogy. Second Edn. 6s.

Cyclopædia of Education; edited by A. E. FLETCHER. With copious Bibliography (34 pp.). Third Edn., 570 pp. Roy. 8vo, 7s. 6d.

De Portugall (Mme.) Synoptical Table of the Kindergarten; on canvas and in cloth case. 2s. 6d.

Essays on the Kindergarten. Ten Lectures read before the Froebel Society. Third Edn. 3s.

Froebel (FRIEDRICH). Autobiography. Edited by EMILE MICHAELIS and H. K. MOORE, B.A. Second Edn. 3s.

—— Letters. Translated and edited by E. MICHAELIS and H. K. MOORE. 3s.

Gilchrist Trust Reports.
BRAMWELL (AMY B.) and HUGHES (H. M.) Training of Teachers. 3s. 6d.
PAGE (MARY H.) Graded Schools. 2s.
BURSTALL (SARA A.) Education of Girls. 3s. 6d.
ZIMMERN (ALICE). Methods of Teaching. 3s. 6d.

Guimps (ROGER DE). Life of Pestalozzi. Edited by J. RUSSELL, B.A. Introduction by Rev. R. H. QUICK. 6s.

—— The Student's Pestalozzi (certain Chapters of the above). 1s. 6d.

Herbart (J. F.) The Science of Education. Translated, with Introduction, by H. M. and E. FELKIN. Preface by OSCAR BROWNING, M.A. Second Edn., revised, with an Index. 4s. 6d.

—— Lectures on Pedagogy. Translated by H. M. and E. FELKIN.
[Shortly.

—— The Application of Psychology to Education. Translated by B. C. MULLINER. [Shortly.

DODD (C. J.) School Method based on Herbartian Principles.
[In press.

FELKIN (H. M. and E.) Introduction to Herbart's "Science of Education." 4s. 6d.

Hewett (M. E. G.) High School Lectures. 3s. 6d.

Malleson (Mrs. F.) Notes on the Early Training of Children. Third Edn. 1s. 6d.; paper, 1s.

Newsholme (Dr. A.) School Hygiene. 29 Figures. Sixth Edn. 2s. 6d.

Peabody (ELIZAB. P.) The Home, The Kindergarten and the Primary School. 3s.

Perez (BERNARD). The First Three Years of Childhood. Preface by Prof. SULLY. 4s. 6d.

THE SCIENCE AND HISTORY OF EDUCATION
(continued)—

Pestalozzi (J. H.) How Gertrude Teaches her Children. Edited by E. COOKE. 3s.

Rein (Prof. W.) Outlines of Pedagogics. 3s.

Richter (JEAN PAUL). Levana. Adapted by SUSAN WOOD, B.Sc. 3s.

Shirreff (EMILY A.) The Kindergarten: Principles of Froebel's System, and their Bearing on the Education of Women. Fifth Edn. 1s. 4d.

Sonnenschein (A.) Foreign Educational Codes relating to Elementary Education. Second Edn., enlarged. 3s. 6d.

—— Specimen Lessons: a Contribution to a Definition of Good Methods of Teaching. 1s.

—— The Truth about Elementary Education. 6d.

Wiebe (Prof. E.) The Paradise of Childhood: a complete Manual of Kindergarten Instruction. Fully illustrated. Fourth Edn. 4to, 7s. 6d. net.

TEXT BOOKS FOR THE KINDERGARTEN.

Baker (AMY). A First History of the English People. Second Edn. Cloth, ea. 1s.
(1) Anglo-Saxons to Henry iii. | (3) James i. to the Revolution.
(2) Edward i. to Elizabeth. | (4) William iii. to Victoria.

Bevan (G. PHILLIPS). Home Geography of England and Wales. 11 Coloured Double-page Maps. 4s. 6d.

Elements of Number. Two parts. Each, 2d.

Mair (Mrs.) Arithmetic for Children. Limp cloth, 1s.

Moore (H. K.) The Child's Pianoforte Book. Illustrated. Third Edn. 4to, 3s. 6d.

—— The Child's Song and Game Book. Parts i. and ii. 4to, ea. 1s.

Mulley (JANE). Songs and Games for Our Little Ones. Third Edn. 1s.

Norton (CAROLINE). Histories for Children. New Illustrated Edns. Cloth, ea. 1s.
(1) Greece.   (2) Rome.   (3) France.

Pullar (A.) Geometry for Kindergarten Students. 499 illustrations. 3s.

Rooper (W. and H.) Illustrated Manual of Object Lessons. 20 Blackboard Illustrations. Third Edn. 3s. 6d.

Sonnenschein (A.) and **Nesbitt** (H. A.) A B C of Arithmetic.
Teacher's Book, two parts, 1s. ea.
Pupil's Book (Exercises), two parts, 4d. ea.

—— Number Pictures for the Nursery, Kindergarten, and School. Sixth Edn. 14 Coloured Sheets. Folio, on one roller, 7s. 6d.; on boards, varnished, 16s. Model Lesson, 6d.

—— Arithmometer.
Box A. Concrete Representations of 1 to 100, 3s. net.
Box B. „   „   100 to 1000, 3s. 6d. net.
Box C. „   „   1000 to 1,000,000. 20s.

SWAN SONNENSCHEIN & CO., LIM., LONDON.